DATE DUE

Condoleezza Rice

AFRICAN-AMERICAN LEADERS

Carol Moseley-Braun

Henry Louis Gates, Jr.

Benjamin Hooks

Eleanor Holmes Norton

Condoleezza Rice

Cornel West

Condoleezza Rice

Gloria Blakely

CHELSEA HOUSE
PUBLISHERS

A Haights Cross Communications Company

Philadelphia

CHELSEA HOUSE PUBLISHERS
VP, NEW PRODUCT DEVELOPMENT Sally Cheney
DIRECTOR OF PRODUCTION Kim Shinners
CREATIVE MANAGER Takeshi Takahashi
MANUFACTURING MANAGER Diann Grasse

Staff for CONDOLEEZZA RICE
EDITOR Sally Cheney
EDITORIAL ASSISTANT Josh Spiegel
PRODUCTION EDITOR Megan Emery
PHOTO EDITOR Sarah Bloom
SERIES & COVER DESIGNER Terry Mallon
LAYOUT Jennifer Krassy Peiler

A Haights Cross Communications ⌁ Company

www.chelseahouse.com

First Printing

1 3 5 7 9 8 6 4 2

Library of Congress Cataloging-in-Publication Data

Blakely, Gloria.
  Condoleezza Rice / Gloria Blakely.
    p. cm. -- (African American leaders)
Includes index.
Summary: A biography of the professor, author, and businesswoman
who became National Security Advisor to President George W. Bush.
 ISBN 0-7910-7683-0
 1. Rice, Condoleezza, 1954---Juvenile literature. 2. National Security
Council (U.S.)--Biography--Juvenile literature. [1. Rice, Condoleezza,
1954- 2. National Security Council (U.S.)--Biography. 3. Women--
Biography. 4. African Americans--Biography.] I. Title. II. Series.
 UA23.15.R53B58 2003
 355'.033073'092--dc22
                                                        2003013660

Table of Contents

INTRODUCTION

Beginning with the publication of the series *Black Americans of Achievement* nearly twenty years ago, Chelsea House Publishers made a commitment to publishing biographies for young adults that celebrated the lives of many of the country's most outstanding African Americans. The mix of individuals whose lives we covered was eclectic, to say the least. Some were well known—Dr. Martin Luther King, Jr., for example—although others we covered might be lesser known—Madam C.J. Walker, for example. Some—like the actor Danny Glover—were celebrities with legions of adoring fans. It mattered not what an individual's "star" quality might be, or how well known they were to the general public. What mattered was the life of the individual—their actions, their deeds, and, ultimately, their influence on the lives of others and our nation, as a whole. By telling the life stories of these unique Americans, we hoped to tell the story of how ordinary individuals are transformed by extraordinary circumstances to people of greatness. We hoped that the special lives we covered would inspire and encourage our young-adult readers to go out in the world and make a positive difference; and judging from the many wonderful letters that we have received over the years from students, librarians, and teachers about our *Black Americans of Achievement* biographies, we are certain that many of our readers did just that!

Now, some twenty years later, we are proud to release this new series of biographies, *African-American Leaders,* which we hope will make a similar mark on the lives of our young-adult readers. The individuals whose lives we cover in this first set of six books are all contemporary

African-American leaders. As these individuals are all living, the biographers made every attempt to interview their subjects so they could provide first-hand accounts and interesting anecdotes about each subject's life.

After reading about the likes of Henry Louis Gates, Jr., Cornel West, Condoleezza Rice, Carol Moseley-Braun, Eleanor Holmes Norton, and Benjamin Hooks, we think you will agree that the lives of these African-American leaders are remarkable. By overcoming the barriers that racism placed in their paths, they are an example of the power and resiliency of the human spirit and an inspiration to us all.

The Editor
Chelsea House Publishers

1

Poise Under Fire

"In the months past, we have been reminded in dramatic and terrifying ways of what happens when difference becomes a license to kill. Terrorism is meant to dehumanize and divide. Growing up in Birmingham, Alabama, I saw the home-grown terrorism of that era. The 1963 bombing of the 16th Street Baptist Church was meant to suck hope out of the future by showing that hope could be killed—child by child. My neighborhood friend, Denise McNair, was killed in that bombing, and though I didn't see it, I heard it a few blocks away. And it is a sound that I can still hear today."

—Condoleezza Rice, commencement speech, Stanford University, *Stanford Report*, June 2002

The date: September 11. Condoleezza Rice, national security advisor to the president of the United States, George W. Bush, strode confidently into her office, not knowing that this was the day that would change the course of her boss's presidency—one hundred eighty degrees according to some. The day seemed to begin just like any other day for Rice: a 6:30 A.M. start, with the end of her workday some fifteen hours later.

Not even when Rice's secretary informed her at 8:45 A.M. that a passenger jet had struck Tower One, the north tower of the World Trade Center in New York City, did she think that the crash was anything more than a horrible accident. Rice was preparing to leave for her daily global briefing with her staff when she heard about Tower One, and did pause for a moment to call President Bush, who was in Florida for a speaking engagement, to inform him of the terrible tragedy. Still, at that time, neither Rice nor the president had reason to believe that the crash was more than an unusual, albeit tragic accident. The Trade Center's twin towers—the highest in the city—had seen close calls in the past.

There was no reason to suspect that the crash was the result of any ill will until Rice's secretary interrupted Rice and her staff at their 9:00 A.M. meeting with a note informing Rice about the crash of yet a second commercial passenger jet—this time the jet had crashed into the Trade Center's south tower, Tower Two. It was then that Rice, the national security advisor to the president, and the rest of America, realized that these two incidents were more than freak accidents. These horrible events were well-orchestrated attacks on America.

The violent acts of terrorism, rebroadcast on every network television station across the country, were hard to

A pensive Condoleezza Rice, stands outside the White House, awaiting the arrival of President George W. Bush, just hours after the terrorist attacks on America on Tuesday, September 11, 2001. Rice, the national security advisor, played an important role in planning the United States government's response to the deadly terrorist attacks.

fathom. With each replay of the commercial airliners tearing through twin bastions of a great nation's financial vibrancy, American viewers had to tell themselves that this was not a stunt in a Hollywood movie. Flames ripping through the buildings and melting their inner cores were all too real. Thousands of lives were lost in the raging fire and smoke. Most of the victims would never be found whole after the skyscapers imploded, falling in massive clouds of rolling dust to the ground.

Within minutes of the second attack, Rice swung into action. Quickly assuming her position in the Situation Room, a basement command center in the West Wing of the White House, Rice made calls to arrange a crisis meeting with National Security Council principals, a select group of presidential appointees responsible for managing the country's safety. She reached the president first. Rather than request his return to the White House, Rice advised President Bush to travel between a variety of secure locations until Washington, D.C. was deemed safe. Rice was talking on the phone and turned around to monitor televised newscasts when reports came in that a third airliner had plowed into the nearby Pentagon, which houses joint U.S. defense headquarters. The shocking news reinforced the fact that time was of the essence.

Following emergency protocol when federal buildings are at risk, Rice joined Vice President Dick Cheney in the secure sublevel command bunker deep beneath the White House complex. From there she continued making calls. Unfortunately, presidential cabinet members and leaders of military and intelligence forces were scattered around the world, so telephone connections had to suffice until in-house assembly became possible. Most importantly, the president and members of his cabinet needed information regarding who was responsible for these heinous acts, for a U.S. response to terror had to be launched quickly. One by one, the members of the cabinet reported in.

Secretary of Defense Donald Rumsfeld, before returning Rice's call, hurried from his office in the Pentagon. He rushed to aid the injured in a smouldering section of the building destroyed by the third plane at 9:43 A.M. General Henry Shelton, chairman of the joint chiefs of staff, the coordinating arm of the nation's military forces, had been winging his way over the Atlantic toward Europe when the attacks occurred. The general redirected the craft homeward, flying over the devastated World Trade Center site. Secretary of State Colin Powell had to conclude prematurely a breakfast discussion in Lima with the president of Peru so he could fly home. George Tenet, director of the Central Intelligence Agency, also responded to Rice's summons.

A WORLD OF CONCERN

As Rice continued to telephone the leaders of allied countries, informing them that the American government was operational, White House and Pentagon staffs evacuated the two premises. The Washington offices of the State and Justice departments and the World Bank were also evacuated. In New York City, the United Nations had cleared its premises, as well.

While the cities of New York and Washington scrambled to respond to their emergency situations, still another commercial jetliner had been commandeered by another group of hijackers, and was now en route to an unknown fourth target. As the country looked on in horror at the prospect of yet another tragic crash, this fourth plane, United flight 93, would meet its own tragic consequences. Recent reports say that the cockpit recorder indicated passengers did not storm the cockpit even though there was no doubt they intended to regain control of the jet. While the passengers' actions cannot be documented, the cockpit recorder does confirm that the hijackers decided to down the plane in western Pennsylvania. No incursion into the cockpit was evident prior to this decision.

Throughout the turmoil brought on by this tragic series of events, America, and indeed the world, came to realize that the great nation of the United States was vulnerable in ways it never dared consider. Words written a decade earlier

Demonstrating her characteristic poise, National Security Advisor Rice answers a barrage of questions from reporters during a briefing at the White House eight days after the terrorist attacks on the Pentagon and the World Trade Center.

by James Baldwin in *The Fire Next Time* aptly describe the internal churnings of many Americans: "Try to imagine how you would feel if you woke up one morning to find the sun shining and all the stars aflame. You would be frightened because it is out of the order of nature. Any upheaval in the universe is terrifying because it so profoundly attacks one's sense of one's own reality." The morning of September 11, 2001 was such a time. It was a time when opposing members of the U.S. Congress stood side by side on the Capitol steps in a display of American solidarity;

when people could not wait to hear the reassuring voices of their loved ones; when normally optimistic Americans were afraid of what tomorrow might bring.

On that fateful occasion, citizens who were saved by quick-thinking action over Pennsylvania, and at ground zero in New York and Washington, as well as everyone else in the nation looked to the U.S. government to restore order to a world believed to have gone mad. Whether people wished for revenge or sought assurances that the violence ultimately would end, the four-pronged attack on American soil triggered a new military directive—a War on Terrorism.

With characteristic composure, Condoleezza Rice orchestrated the planning process for a lengthy siege unlike any other. She helped shape Bush's press statement to the nation at 9:30 that morning. She coordinated daily meetings with National Security Council members. At a White House press briefing almost one week after the tragic events, Rice became the public barometer of the president's perspective on foreign policy. She explained to the media in what is seen as her signature selfless style: "I think the president is going to use this opportunity [an upcoming speech] to talk about the sustained nature of this campaign, that this cannot be a campaign that is thought of like the Gulf War, where there was a capital with a leadership that one understood fully in a way that we traditionally understood leadership." The White House immediately embarked on a war of intelligence, a war on bank accounts, and one of toppling the terrorist stronghold in Afghanistan.

In response to a reporter's question, Rice added, "I think that every American understands that life changed on September 11th. Now what didn't change is our way of life. And, as the president said when he welcomed workers back here at the White House Complex, it's every American's duty to try to get back to doing the things that make us American: Going to work and going to shop and taking your kids to school."

"But," she said, "there is no doubt that the country faced a severe shock and blow" from which some adaptation had to arise. In addition to ratcheting up her advisory role with the cabinet and as presidential confidant, before the entire world each week Rice easily donned the shoes of key spokesperson on behalf of the president of the United States. Terrorism was recognizable ground to her. Rice had come of age in a place where strident and often violent acts erupted to maintain the segregated status quo between European and African Americans. Her youth represented a time when differences in skin color and continental origin made an entire race of people a target.

2

Learning to Soar

"My parents, I think they are extraordinary. Of all people, what they achieved and what they were able to pass on to me was extraordinary."
—Condoleezza Rice, from Wilkerson,
"The Most Powerful Woman in the World,"
Essence, February 2002

Condi, as Rice is called by friends and family, readily took to her middle-class life in Titusville, a section of segregated Birmingham, Alabama. Her family did their best to isolate her from particularly harsh realities below the Mason-Dixon Line, where governing bodies treated racial dominance more seriously. Southern officials upheld detailed laws that outlined how blacks and whites must lead separate lives in schools, churches, houses, marriages, and restaurants, how they must maintain inflexible distances in bus seating and so much more.

If there was any doubt about the rules, "Colored Only" and "White Only" signs were posted liberally to set the record straight. Failing that, a mere look of displeasure or choice words of guidance would either put the offending black person in his or her place, or foreshadow a possible lynching that could bring the individual's freewheeling episode to a gruesome deadly end.

Condi's parents, John and Angelena, insulated her from the racial intolerance swirling around them. By rarely having contact with white Americans, the former racial pattern of cowering to inequitable social codes was replaced with her confidence in being the best among the black elite. This status had been clearly modeled through several generations of college-educated forebearers.

On her father's side of the family, just one generation out of plantation slavery in Green County, free-born John Jr., better known as Grandaddy Rice to Condi, emerged from sharecropping a Eutaw, Alabama cotton field. With his pride well intact and enough money earned for college tuition, Condi's grandfather set out to find where a colored man could get educated in 1918 America. Grandaddy Rice enrolled in the church-operated Stillman Institute in Tuscaloosa. After a year of "book learning," however, his supply of cotton money earnings ran out, and he asked how the other boys remained in college for longer periods of time. He was informed of the scholarship program available to would-be Presbyterian ministers. The arrangement sounded pretty good to Grandaddy Rice, even if he was Methodist.

Having completed his education successfully and having spent a period of time starting a family in Baton Rouge, Louisiana, the church assigned him to Birmingham, where he established the Westminster Presbyterian ministry. Being

The Stillman Institute in Tuscaloosa, Alabama was one of the few schools of higher learning in the South that admitted African Americans in the early 1900s. John Rice, Condoleezza's grandfather, received his education at the Institute.

a practical spiritual leader for his flock, he made a point to send young men from the congregation to the Stillman Institute each year. In doing so, he hoped to show teenagers that the color of one's skin does not have to be worn as shackles, because the human spirit knows no bounds. Grandaddy Rice was intent on handing African-American children the keys to a better life; and a lack of funds or some other momentary setback was not going to deter him. At home his expectations soared even higher for his own children, and they did not disappoint him. Each child found individual paths to the colleges of their choice. His son John Wesley, Condi's father, pursued an academic path, first entering his dad's Birmingham ministry. Then it was on to graduate school, after which he would take a position at the University of Denver.

The Rays, from whom Condi's mother descended had an equally impressive and fearless legacy. The family matriarch was a house slave similar to the matriarch of the Rice side of the family. Condi's great-grandfather, however, was the ruling white slave owner, and, as such, Condi's great-grandmother was exposed to educational tools and creature comforts in her slave home. Like Grandaddy Rice, Condi's great-grandmother had high expectations for her mulatto children. Like the Rices, the Ray children met those expectations. Two daughters graduated from the well-known Tuskegee Institute fully trained in nursing. Albert Ray, Condi's grandfather, transformed manual labor in three industries (mining contractor, blacksmith, and housing construction) into material comfort. Albert Ray was a proud man, who made it his business to shelter his family from *Jim Crow* laws dividing the races. For example, he preferred that his children avoid using public restrooms designated "colored," he elected to buy a car with his hard-earned cash, so his family and he did not have to suffer the indignities of segregated buses. When one of his sons landed a much sought-after factory job up north in Pittsburgh, Pennsylvania, Albert Ray retrieved the young man and returned him to his first priority—college.

Those strong family traditions could not help becoming a part of Condoleezza's character through both word and deed. Shielded by her middle-class enclave, Condi learned the prevailing system of widespread prejudice in many ways limited racists, not her. Achieving her goals by being twice as knowledgeable and working twice as hard as whites was a universal defense mechanism espoused by most black communities for many generations. But in the Rice household it literally meant you had the power to achieve any professional goal chosen. You could become president.

PREPARING FOR LIFE

From the day of Condi's birth on Sunday morning November 14, 1954, Condi's parents systematically prepared her to face the world on her terms outside *Jim Crow* rule. It was the same year the Supreme Court ruling on *Brown v. Board of Education* began tearing down the premise that separate is equal. National adherence to the landmark ruling was systematically tested and found wanting.

Condi's parents, Angelena and John, did not join mass demonstrations for equal rights after Rosa Parks, living seventy miles south in Montgomery, reignited the modern civil rights movement by refusing to give her bus seat to a white man in December 1955. Reverend Fred Shuttlesworth did pick up freedom's light in Birmingham and with it launched a protracted campaign against racial discrimination. Although the Rices recognized the benefits of the movement and supported boycotts, political activism was not their personal answer to white racism—Condi was. Her parents were excellent teachers who used their training to Condi's advantage. She was taught to excel at talents supposedly reserved for the ruling class—classical music, foreign languages, literature, the list went on.

Formal education began at age three, when the family discovered how special Condi was. The preschooler wanted to learn to play the piano so loved by three generations of older women in her family. Despite some reservations about her youth, Angelena, who taught music and science to high schoolers, and Grandmother Mattie, a home-based music instructor, started Condi's training in the unusual combination of the classics and gospel. Little Condi, whose name was created from the Italian musical instruction, *con dolcezza*, meaning "with sweetness," could play from sheet music before she could read words. Her first recital arrived quickly. The four-year-old sat at the piano in a taffeta dress with a tam tastefully adorning her head and delivered "A Doll's Funeral," which she refers to as a small Tchaikovsky knockoff. The listeners at the tea party to welcome Birmingham public school teachers must have spread the word about the child prodigy because, in addition to regular Sunday appearances in her father's church, demand for local performances remained constant for six or seven years. Condi soaked up the discipline needed to fulfill her pianist obligations; that is, the required lessons and practice time on top of other interests in children's clubs, ballet lessons, youth groups, and Sunday services at her father's church, Westminster Presbyterian.

By age five, her literary skills had caught up with her musical and social talents. However, when the principal of the elementary school refused to enroll Condi until she reached the appropriate age, Angelena resolved this impasse with home schooling. Angelena took a year's leave of absence from Fairfield Industrial High School to immerse Condi in study techniques befitting a president. Angelena established a high level of self-discipline that the child would never forget. There was no playtime built into her school day. Among other techniques employed: a speed-reading machine swept Condi through her books, and Angelena worked with her constantly to enhance her memory of music, English, and art. By the time Condi was eight years old, French lessons in reading and comprehension were added to a rather refined syllabus of extracurricular studies. Just as Condi understood and wanted full immersion in the ways of the larger world, her local friends grew to understand that it would be a long wait each night before Condi could giggle childishly with them during jump rope and other outdoor games.

Condi craved educational challenges, and the praise and recognition that followed when she met the challenges head on. In time, as her prodigy status became less unique and as demand for her appearances faded, family piano lessons, her first challenge, lost their thrill. She seriously considered quitting. But seeing the bigger picture of a concert career, her mother coaxed Condi into the Birmingham Southern Conservatory of Music, where she was one of the first African Americans to benefit from its new policy of integration in 1965. The creative environment generously dappled with student competitions and artistic experimentation catapulted Condi's existing abilities to new heights and broadened her musical experiences to include the flute and violin. She began to share her mother's dream of a concert career. Angelena could breathe a sigh of relief, for the Rice plan was moving along at breakneck speed.

"My parents were very strategic. I was going to be so well prepared," Rice recalled, "and I was going to do all of these things that were revered in white society so well, that I would be armored somehow from racism. I would be able to confront white society on its own terms."

Angelena's belief in her child ran deeper than external perceptions. She referred to her as a genius following a battery of psychological tests at Southern University in Baton Rouge. Today Condi says that she has observed real genius at Stanford University, and she is not it. At best she saw herself as an above average student. But Angelena's goal was to allow her child the opportunity to live up to her God-given potential and praise her progress along the way. Her parent's loving gift of unshakable knowledge and the skill to apply it led Condoleezza to skip the second and seventh grades early in life. To Condi, experiencing a new discipline meant more than a casual fling, she felt compelled to become good at whatever was undertaken. Nothing less than the excellence of being counted among the best was satisfactory to the young A student.

This competitive spirit also applied to sports. Hours spent on Sunday afternoons, nuzzled beside her father watching football on television while insightful play-by-play critique from her "coach dad" rocked Condi with blissful joy. The youngster developed a genuine fanaticism for sports. From the age of four, John equipped his little girl with intimate knowledge of athletic challenges. The ability to churn out a first-rate-showing in the family "Rice Bowl" each Thanksgiving was one example of Daddy's handiwork. Gridiron wars became so much a part of her makeup that Condi decided to marry a football player when she grew up.

Being raised in a religious household by Reverend and Mrs. Rice also balanced Condi's firebrand spirit with graceful self-assurance cupped in a happy generous nature. A special energy, particularly from Reverend Rice, buoyed the inner spirit of his family and Westminster congregation. At the same time, he strove to make a difference in the economic lives of neighborhood children by establishing the first Head Start program in Birmingham in 1965 and guiding boys to a taste of leadership in the Boys Scouts. John's commitment extended to instilling his well-rounded counseling, ministry, and teaching experiences in the Birmingham Youth Opportunity Center, which placed black children in part-time employment and summer jobs. Then during after-school and weekend youth fellowship, the Reverend exposed African-American high school students to chess and a host of athletic games, as well as the arts. Teachers organized to participate in the fellowship also gave their students a chance to fine-tune their academics in preparation for college.

RACISM—IT IS WHAT IT IS

Life proceeded smoothly in the separate, but multi-dimensional world of middle-class Titusville where Condi's parents pushed the limits for their only child. During moments when parallel universes between African Americans and European Americans did intersect, Angelena Rice showed her daughter how to command respect from white society. Early in the 1960s, Angelena and Condi went shopping. While her mother made a purchase, Condi explored the store's other goodies. The youngster must have touched something because the saleswoman commanded her to keep her hands off a hat. Angelena wasted no time stepping up and teaching the woman respect by instructing her daughter to touch every hat in the store.

On another occasion in a downtown store, Condi asked to try on a dress, this time as tradition dictated the salesperson pointed her to the storage room used by coloreds. Angelena would not have her daughter treated in such an undignified manner. She reminded the woman that she could take her money to a place offering better services. Probably not wanting to see her commission exit with Angelena, the saleswoman showed Condi to the back of the fitting room and stood watch outside the stall, presumably to ensure that no one discovered her breach of racial etiquette. Through example augmented by instruction, Angelena showed her daughter how to navigate through an often unfair world with her grace, poise, and dignity intact.

Even though laws against segregation in public places were being overturned this remained a dangerous time to move the lines of socially acceptable behavior between races. Her mother's lessons in respect and self-confidence during the 1960s could have ended quite differently. The lengths to which some people resisted change were clearly evident in the churches splintered by bombings across the South. Some locals say police supported the ensuing neighborhood attacks by clearing the streets before the Ku Klux Klan, a group promoting white supremacy, came through sporting shotguns and bombs.

Those unabashed acts of hatred probably forced the silent segment in 1963 Birmingham to decide if it truly wanted to harbor such violence in its midst. In no time, the majority of citizens voted then Public Safety Commissioner Bull Connors and his cronies out of office, but the lame duck administration refused to give up power. Both sets of officials tried to manage the city in separate sessions until the court determined who would rule. That municipal instability made an already difficult environment highly volatile.

Several bombs thrown at the Rices' neighborhood failed to detonate, but Condi's friend Anthony Shore's home was not so fortunate. Nor was the 16th Street Baptist Church on September 15, 1963, when it was shattered by an explosion felt miles away. Earlier that year, the Baptist church had been headquarters to "Project C," involving Martin Luther King, Jr. and other top civil rights activists. Their nonviolent sit-ins and boycotts of downtown businesses landed many of those activists in jail. During King's period of incarceration he penned the now famous *Letter from a Birmingham Jail,* which elegantly described group tactics and deep-rooted motivations of the unrelenting cry for just treatment. Their persistence began to hurt the cash registers of local businesses and drew Birmingham City officials to the negotiation table.

Within months, Project C demonstrators had gained significant concessions from downtown business people, who agreed to integrate lunch counters and hire some black clerks in their stores. The city seemed further divided after the settlement was reached, however. Following a riot-torn summer, some white citizens, who were likely resentful of the concessions brought about by the 16th Street Baptist Church's Project C group, plotted retaliation.

Several girls attending Sunday school in the lower level of the church did not suspect that the mere act of going to the bathroom would put them in the path of an explosion that cut short their lives. Of the four youngsters who died, three were well known to Condi. Denise McNair was Condi's eleven-year-old-friend. Her father's photography, documenting birthdays, weddings and a host of celebratory events, made him a much-loved fixture in Titusville. Cynthia Wesley, a teen just three years older than Condi, lived on property abutting the Rices'. Young Addie Mae Collins had been a member of the homeroom staffed by Condi's uncle. Condi reflected on those times, "I think it was a face of hatred that had a kind of searing impact on children." Those children would be adults before the gavel of justice convicted three of the four murderers in 1977, 2001 and 2002. The fourth alleged perpetrator died before charges were filed.

The tragic events of the 1963 bombing rocked the entire country. Condi was only nine years old at the time of the tragedy. The sight of the small coffins that held the bodies of her friends would bring much sadness to Condi and, perhaps, fear—the fear that Birmingham was an unsafe place. The intensity of that feeling lasted only a short time, hoever, becauseof Condi's faith in her parents' ability to protect her from American terrorism. Given the brutality involved, it is hard to imagine how any parent could soothe a frightened child into a sense of safety, but desperate times required heroic measures. If the city's police force would not do their job of guarding black Alabamans, then the men residing in threatened neighbor-hoods would. Black men, Condi's minister father included, policed their communities with weapons at their sides.

Leading up to that day, Condi had followed with great interest news reports of Public Safety Commissioner Bull Connor's violent reactions to civil rights initiatives. Exercising his authority over the fire and police depart-ments, Connor had the protesting African-American teenagers slammed to their knees by the force of pressurized water from firehoses. During one demonstration the force of the water barrage literally stripped the bark off unmoving trees firmly rooted in the park. The same young protesters were bloodied by police dogs set upon them, and still demonstrations continued. The civil rights movement could not be washed away.

News of the movement filled Condi with daily questions. Her parents always explained the transpiring actions carefully and as objectively as they would to an adult. Her father, in particular, added historical meaning and clarified the basic goals of the activism seen on television. The movement's immediate objective was to eradicate the legal impediments that kept people of color, women, and individuals of certain religious denominations from enjoying their full rights as citizens of the United States. (Their objective would eventually be achieved with the introduction of the 1964 Comprehensive Civil Rights Act.) The ultimate goal, however, focused on taking race out of the equation in the competition for wealth, housing, education, and all aspects of society that keep a country whole. The Act endeavored to ensure that all of America become a color blind society, judging individuals solely on their merit.

More recently Condi said, "The fact of the matter is race matters in America. It has, it always has. Maybe there will be a day when it doesn't, but I suspect that it will for a long time to come. It matters in different ways today than it did in 1963 in Birmingham. But it still matters." And yet, "talking about it as if it is an impediment that cannot be overcome by hard work and access to education and all those things" is an injustice to American children.

A few days after President Johnson signed the 1964 bill into law, the Rices took a small step to reinforce gains made by grassroots protest across the nation. They clearly showed which side of the movement they favored by sitting down in a previously whites-only restaurant amid stares, but without incident. Assuming their place in the restaurant represented progress toward a freer tomorrow. Sensing there were many paths to social change from passive resistance to outright intimidation, the Rices typically opted for the middle ground. They quietly prepared their daughter and other community children to be so culturally and academically sophisticated in the forthcoming integrated nation that it would be impossible to deny them their rightful position. Used in that manner, education became a tool of liberation.

3

Life Outside Birmingham

> People often ask, 'Is it [music] relaxing?' Struggling with Brahms is not relaxing. But it is completely transporting. You cannot hold Brahms and something else in your head at the same time. And, so it gets you out of whatever world you're in and into another world, and I really love that."
> —Condoleezza Rice, from Wilkerson, "The Most Powerful Woman in the World," *Essence*, February 2002

Racial segregation excluded teachers Angelena and John Rice from a graduate degree program at the nearby University of Alabama. So they packed their car during school vacations and hit the road to see the world far north of Birmingham. A Rice-style road trip entailed the usual nonstop drive out of the South followed by pauses at a number of northern college campuses and historic sites. One stop outside the White House when Condi was ten years old prompted her to state with upmost sincerity, "Daddy, I'm barred out of there now because of the color of my skin. But one day, I'll be in that house." Before that day would become a reality for Rice, however, the family would make a pit stop in Colorado, where Angelena and John would take graduate courses in education at the University of Denver. The young Condi would enjoy her time in Denver, taking ice skating lessons, and basking in a peaceful universe that seemed a million miles away from the unsettling heat of her hometown, which had aptly earned the label—Bombingham.

Then in 1965, John received an offer he could not refuse. This time their car transported his family and him sixty miles to Tuscaloosa, Alabama to become dean of Stillman College—the very place where Grandaddy Rice had originated the family's college and religious traditions. Long gone were the institution's days solely as a training ground for black ministers. Stillman had evolved since then into a fully accredited, four-year college offering a variety of academic majors. This new position at Stillman would, ultimately, pave the way to an administrative position at the University of Denver three years later. After earning his Master of Arts in Education on June 10, 1969 from the University of Denver, John was offered, and gladly accepted, the position of assistant director of admission at Denver.

Although race relations were changing, a full professorship that would have provided the family with more income and tenure was not in the cards for John. He nevertheless shaped his own opportunity by creating a program called the "Black Experience in America" for instruction to university students. His teaching eventually broadened to include worthy speakers, such as Howard Robinson, executive director of the Congressional Black Caucus and Reverend Channing Philips, the first black man nominated to run for president.

Fannie Lou Hamer formed the Mississippi Freedom Democratic Party in the 1960s to pressure the traditional Democratic Party to address the concerns of African Americans. Ms. Hamer (seen here) is one of Condoleezza Rice's heroes.

John's dedication to African-American studies, and his own sharing of in-depth personal experiences seldom represented in American history, spurred the university to assign him a new title, adjunct history professor.

John's university positions exposed his young daughter to hosts of black luminaries visiting the university. Fannie Lou Hamer was one such person. "I will never forget meeting a woman named Fannie Lou Hamer when I was a teenager," Condoleezza told the 2002 graduating class at Stanford University. "She came to the University of Denver to speak to my father's class. She was not sophisticated in the way we think of it, yet so compelling that I remember the power of her message even today. In 1964, Fannie Lou Hamer refused to listen to those who told her that a sharecropper with a sixth-grade education could not, or should not, launch a challenge that would dismantle the racist infrastructure of Mississippi's Democratic Party. She did it anyway."

"And Ms. Hamer reminds us that heroes are not born," extolled Rice, "they are made; and they come from unlikely places. There are countless other everyday heroes whose deeds are less dramatic but no less important."

Her parents settled into a house located in the Englewood section of South Denver. While Angelena continued teaching and became an assistant in the Admissions Office, this rarefied, yet familiar northwestern air took on a bold new dimension for the young, black, gifted child from the South. Condi was smack in the middle of the white world for which she had been carefully groomed. It was her age to fly, and nothing was going to stop her. For the first time, she was placed in private school, St. Mary's Academy near the University of Denver's campus. Many of John's colleagues enrolled their children in this school, which was noted for its well-rounded college preparation in foreign languages and other essential academics. The secondary grades were all girls, and with the addition of Condi, only four of the seventy young ladies in her class were black. Clearly she was not in Titusville anymore.

One of the youngest sophomores after skipping two prior grades, Condi—an A student—started off the school year listening to a counselor say that her intelligence test scores indicated she was not college material. It was an old refrain heard by generation after generation of African Americans. While this type of assessment stymied the aspirations of many young impressionable minds, Condi's parents both knew the systematic game being played and knew a potential college student when they saw one. Angelena simply told Condi the counselor was wrong and to ignore the statement. That was not a hard thing for the young girl to do with an interesting array of activities in front of her. She looked forward to ice skating all year, continued music lessons at the school, and added tennis to her competitive repertoire.

Besides, she was never the type to be distracted by self-reflection or worry about uninvited opinions. No doubt her family's discipline had rendered Condi undeterred by any suggestions of incompetence. She sailed through high school and extracurricular activities. In her, teachers found that unusual package of a well-mannered, confident, and charming young lady, who was imminently teachable and coachable. By the end of her junior year, Condi had enough credits to graduate.

CONTINUING THE LEGACY

Her parents advised their daughter to enroll in college at the start of the school year. Instead Condi wanted to experience the social norm of receiving a diploma with her graduating class. Angelena and John were adamant about not losing the competitive advantage Condi held over her peers. They insisted she enter college. Now this could have escalated into a showdown of immense proportions; but the rebellion cascading through the young populace in the 1960s and '70s never appealed to Condi. Loosely formed notions of flower children, free love, drugs, or "down with the establishment and up with communes" did not feel right for her. Likewise, defiance of parental authority would fly in the face of the respect Angelena and John had shown her over the years, and the respect Condi had for her heritage.

The Rice family found common ground, however, when Condi promised to do both. She began two courses at the University of Denver on an academic scholarship while finishing her senior year at St. Mary's—all this in addition to continuing with her piano skills, writing articles for the school newspaper, and competing in pairs skating. To receive a high school diploma with her classmates and stroll into the prom on the arm of a college man was awesome for her.

Beginning college at age fifteen must have been just as exciting for this seeker of educational stimuli. Condi's first college course put her face to face with William Shockley's theories about the genetically inferior culture and intellect of Africans and their descendants. Condi could not sit quietly and let that highly critical assessment pass unchallenged. She suggested there was evidence to the contrary. When the lecturing professor stated no such evidence existed, she assailed him with an irrefutable truth, "I'm the one who speaks French! I'm the one who plays Beethoven. I am better at your culture than you are." She told the learned professor that culture can be taught and obviously has nothing to do with whether you are or are not black. That was the day she truly understood her parents' strategy, which she continued to apply with a vengeance. Condi followed up her point by "acing" the course and taking her inherited gifts as far as they would go.

Being up at 4:30 in the morning on a typical weekday got her to the practice rink by 6:30 A.M. to work on skating four hours before attending honors classes. Years later, Condi said she persisted at skating despite a lack of raw talent for the sport and despite her mother's concern that she would injure her hands. She figured that the risk was worth it, given the sense of excitement she felt participating in this competitive sport. After polishing her musical skills at night, those long activity-filled days often ended with studying. Admittedly she was more disciplined at skating and music practice than her nightly studies, but her sometimes lackadaisical attitude did not diminish Condi's ability to ace exams. Still in globe-trotting adulthood, filled with the fantastic sights and sounds of renowned foreign places, she wished more could be remembered about those sites beyond the vague impressions left by the last minute cramming sessions in her youth.

MUSICAL DETOUR

Despite procrastinating tendencies, while at the University of Denver, her strategy of excellence proceeded like clockwork until she cashed in an unexpected reality check during the summer following her sophomore year. Luckily she had acquiesced to her father's demand that she attend a full-fledged college, rather than a performance school, such as her beloved Juilliard, for in Aspen her dreams of the concert stage came crashing down on Condi and her friend, Darcy Taylor. They both studied at the Lamont School of Music where they were considered high-ly talented. But pitted against younger contestants at the acclaimed Aspen Music Festival, Condi and Darcy watched eleven-year-olds play classic compositions beautifully from sight, and clearly without needing the year of practice it had taken the two of them. The young ladies instantly knew who would grace the world stage performing before thousands of people, and who would be left aside to teach music.

Condi did not want to be known as a very good pianist. To reach the top of her field she had to be among the best. If she could not hope to become an outstanding concert musi-cian, she would have to change her major. It was just difficult to imagine what that would be. Possibly for the first time in her life she was left without a plan or passion driving her next move. Her parents, who had invested an enormous amount

Young scholar: Condoleezza Rice poses for a picture at the University of Denver. In 1974, she graduated cum laude and Phi Beta Kappa with a bachelor's degree in political science.

of time and money in her music education, accepted the news well. They knew their daughter had a good head on her shoulders and was capable of making wise choices. Their only desire was her graduating within the original plan of four years. Condi, on the other hand, kept thinking about the cost of music lessons and the thirteen-thousand-dollar Chickering grand piano purchased to eliminate her nightly walks from the campus practice room. The American Chickering grands, rivaling Steinways, were first crafted in 1840 and rose to international acclaim.

4

A Rising Star

"In my talk to you and the incoming graduate students,
I gave you some unsolicited advice. And because I was
provost, you had no choice but to listen. It seems that
now you are going out the same way that you came in.
Back then, I said that your job here was to find your
passion. Not just something that interested you, but
something that you couldn't live without."

—Condoleezza Rice, Commencement
speech, Stanford University,
Stanford Report, June 2002

With the help of John Rice, Condi's friend, Darcy Taylor, obtained a university scholarship and started a landscape company while taking business courses. Condi, on the other hand, entered her junior year a woman in search of a driving force. How different this was from a similar period in high school when she raced ahead of a family game plan. She

Professor Josef Korbel at the University of Denver in 1975. Dr. Korbel sparked Condoleezza Rice's lifelong interest in international politics.

switched her college major to "undeclared" and explored a wide range of subjects from which she hoped to find inspiration. English Literature seemed too "squishy" and ethereal. Government studies at the structural level involving voting, political parties, and such was a bore and did not satisfy her thirst for a challenge. That is, until she enrolled in Professor Josef Korbel's "Introduction to International Politics."

Korbel was one of a number of high echelon diplomats who fled post-World War II upheavals in Europe, which redefined sovereign borders and established Cold War enmity around the world. The demands of the new Soviet-United States stress points compelled American universities to create disciplined studies that looked at the changing international arena. Professor Korbel's background made him especially well prepared to shed dynamic international light on the University of Denver. He was not your average refugee; he served under Czechoslovak President Jan Masaryk. Just before the Communists seized control of the country in 1948, Korbel received a new position on a special United Nations (U.N.) commission. It did not take him long to decide to leave the Communist takeover behind. Upon arriving in the United States with a family that included daughter Madeleine, Korbel boldly assumed his post at the U.N. headquarters in New York City—that is, until the reformed Czech government pressured him out the following year. Korbel departed its employ and rebounded in a different vocation, teaching Soviet studies with political colleagues on the campuses of Oxford, Harvard, Columbia, MIT, and, of course, the University of Denver. Where other government courses failed to interest Condi, constantly shifting international sands and the first-hand expertise of Korbel's instruction on the Soviet Union set off a spark. Condi has quipped that hearing about Russian leader Josef Stalin's policy swings in the 1920s was like falling in love. She wanted to absorb as much about Russian life and their military conquests as humanly possible.

She did not keep her intentions a secret from the professor. Korbel nurtured her obvious inquisitiveness much like a father would who was preparing a child for a lifetime of political research and analysis. His encouragement of Condi surprised colleagues who knew Korbel disapproved of women in the school's graduate government studies program. Apparently overcoming his bias, Korbel would establish a working relationship with Condi that was strong; so strong that Condi describes Korbel in paternal terms. Given the familial closeness that Condi and Korbel shared, it's not surprising that their academic studies frequently spilled over into the Korbel home, sometimes in the form of rousing dinner discussions with Madeleine Albright. (Years later, Albright would follow in her father's political footsteps—first as U.N. Ambassador in the Carter administration and later as secretary of state during the Clinton presidency.)

In the Rice household, political expression was the order of the day. Condi's father, John entered local government and represented Denver on the Foreign Service Generalist Selection Board in Washington, D.C. Many years later in 1978, he was appointed to the Denver Urban Renewal Authority. "Daddy's little star," without knowing it, was on the path to moving the family's government legacy to higher ground. She says that she did not plan the outstanding positions to which she would climb. It was more a matter of plunging into subjects that she adored and being open to the possibilities her expertise brought.

For the moment, Russian studies had her attention in school and out. She completed her basic undergraduate courses, but wanted more on the subject than her two years of study supplied. At the age of nineteen, she had already mastered the Russian language with its Cyrillic alphabet that confounded many scholars. A reward for all the hard work was departing the University of Denver as one of its most honored undergraduate women in the class of 1974. She walked away cum laude with a Bachelor of Arts degree. She was named Phi Beta Kappa, won the Political Science Honor Award, was a member of the female seniors honorary Mortar Board, and was named Outstanding Senior Woman. These achievements paved her entrance to Notre Dame University in Indiana.

GRAD SCHOOL

Condi liked the conservative values of Roman Catholic Notre Dame. The acquaintance her father had with Rev. Theodore Hesburgh, then-president of the school, gave her a deeper perspective on its merger of God's mission of service with academic strength. From all those summer trips to college campuses, Condi already knew the university had a notable Department of Government and International Studies. The department was created by Hungarian émigré Stephen D. Kertesz, a former diplomat who, like her earlier mentor, Korbel, had fled his Communist-ruled homeland.

Condi really had no long-term career goal in mind at the start of the master's program. A compulsion for Russia propelled her and her new mentor, Professor George Brinkley, to create a plan of action that matched her academic strengths and would hold her interest. Unlike many students entering the program, Condi had more than a passing knowledge of Soviet history and literature. Although her undergrad courses on the subject were cursory, she had the benefit of Professor Korbel's experience with Communism. Additional instruction in the Russian language provided cultural nuances that gave her a fuller appreciation of untranslated literature. Russian novels with dark tragic undercurrents represented only a portion of the self-study that had already shaped her understanding of culture in the USSR (United Soviet Socialist Republic).

Brinkley soon recognized that Condi's devotion to her studies needed no more outside stimulation than the challenges of learning at a clip fast enough to keep up with her intellectual appetite. A specialized program allowed Condi the freedom of directed readings that emphasized independent research along with fewer basic courses. So essentially her learning was accelerated by small class sizes and a tremendous amount of one-on-one attention by Professor Brinkley. He saw in Condi, a student able to master the Russian language far more easily than he, the award-winning Soviet scholar, had in his student years. However, she did lift her head out of her books quite often during her first year away from home. Another plus from her specialized curriculum was a lack of morning classes. That and the ability to soak in her studies quickly gave Condi plenty of time to enjoy the discos in the city of South Bend, Indiana. Partying through the night until 5:00 A.M. was a regular occurrence for the young rock and rhythm & blues music lover. This was her time to let her hair down with friends without jeopardizing her graduate work.

In due course, Condi completed her master's program with concepts by Hans Morgenthau and the added influence of Zbigniew Brzezinski and John Erickson fashioning her research paper. Condi's pragmatic nature had dismissed ideological theories of international relations in favor of the thinking behind *realpolitik*. *Realpolitik* espouses that both order and chaos between nations are functions of basic human needs to thrive and survive. Therefore alliances and wars are products of national self-interest and the values surrounding those interests. As one consequence, military force by threat or deed set the parameters for the contest between competing international powers.

Looking back on Condi's year at Notre Dame, Brinkley believes it brought greater focus to her passion and set her on track for the strategic government work that awaited her. Surprisingly at the time, she had a different career path in mind. Condi felt ready to earn a living and was offered a job at the technology giant, Honeywell. The offer fell through, when the company reorganized, however. Law school became the backup plan. She was accepted into several programs, but postponed entering at the behest of Professor Korbel.

POST GRADUATE LIFE

Condi continued the strategy research started in her master's paper at Notre Dame. Korbel thought her talent for global issues would be wasted in the practice of law, and should be cultivated and shared with a larger audience in academia. Before deciding what to do with the rest of her life, she opened her mind to the idea of a teaching career by beginning a few courses at the Graduate School of International Studies (GSIS) in 1975. In doing so, she said "I realized that I liked political science more than law, and I sort of stumbled into a Ph.D. program." Both Korbel and Brinkley lent their support to her doctoral work that officially got underway in 1976.

Living with her parents again restored her comfortable routine going to church and watching the all-consuming football games with Dad and college friends. Those televised kick-offs seen at the Rice house were usually accompanied with plenty of merriment and often loaded with spicy gumbo. "I've managed to have a wide circle of friends. Some are from my university days. Some of them I watch sports with. Sports is a big element in my life. Football, hockey, basketball, sumo wrestling, anything with a score. I love the competition."

To stroke her financial and musical strings, Condi began giving piano lessons in addition to practicing regularly. Meanwhile the GSIS at Denver was heavily salted with illustrious scholars, who had a wide range of experiences in international planning organizations and universities around the world. Their collective expertise formed a spectrum of study much broader than the Cold War politics found in other university programs. GSIS covered economic, social, and cultural interactions both within and between national borders around the globe, thus giving Condi the depth she needed in Soviet military dynamics greatly augmented by the sociological tone brewing behind the scenes.

Those six years of post-graduate study came during an amazing international chess game and a lack of Russian masters of the female persuasion to anticipate the plays. Her research carried Condi through the proliferation of nuclear weaponry and diplomatic efforts to contain such devices to the dueling superpowers—consisting of the United States and the USSR. Sequentially along the broad picture, the Helsinki Accords legitimized post-World War II borders of European countries. Cold War rhetoric thawed sufficiently for the Apollo-Soyuz space link to get off the ground and for the sale of U.S. grain to the Soviets. Then attitudes stiffened again after the Soviets invaded Afghanistan.

Condi was no less curious and opinionated about the history unfolding in her field of study than during the progress of the civil rights movement in her childhood. Her growing knowledge of the Russian mind made her conclusions about the correct American response to the Soviet incursion into Afghanistan just as strong as those about Bull Connor's violent reactions to peaceful civil disobedience in Birmingham many years prior. Specifically, she thought President Carter's strategy was a pretty lame attempt to prevent further Soviet expansion into oil-rich nations of the Middle East. She expected a reaction more telling than a U.S. reduction in the flow of agricultural products and technology to Russia. She wanted to see something more pronounced than a political slap on Soviet wrists by delaying the SALT II treaty and boycotting the Moscow Summer Olympics. Her faith in the Democratic Party was severely shaken by those decisions.

Supporters of Carter's restraint might have found the attitude of scholarly émigrés and the generations of thought molded by their lessons on the USSR aggressor a bit one-sided. His reaction to the Russian central government was not clothed in the enmity of a people defeated by Soviet military forces. Whatever Carter's reason for tempered action, Condi could not see it. Prior to casting her ballot in the 1980 election, she registered as a Republican and, accordingly, gave Ronald Reagan her vote of approval. "I was a registered Democrat and might never have changed parties were it not for what I thought was our mishandling of the Cold War," Condi explained. Her father had been a Republican for years, but his reasons had more to do with Dixiecrats (Democrat segregationists) at home refusing to register him to vote simply because of his race.

Condi pressed on with her studies gaining a conservative world view in the chilly atmosphere of two dominant political powers. Through her dissertation she formulated unique research on the lesser-known subject of the Czech military and the widespread impact on its homeland. The work took her to the Pentagon where she interned in 1977, the same year Josef Korbel died of stomach cancer. Then with an internship at a distinguished political think-tank, The Rand Corporation, she continued down the path that her mentor, Korbel, had encouraged her to walk. Numerous trips to Moscow and St. Petersburg during the years spent on her doctorate also brought an enormous dimension of reality to her research. Some of her estimations were later verified in meetings with Soviet officials. "At one point in my life, I knew more about the Soviet general staff than the Soviet general staff knew about itself," Condi recalls. "I know this because I sat next to the former chief of the Soviet general staff who kept saying, 'how did you know that?'" Giving further emphasis to her growing skills in that educational period, she added reading Czech to the foreign languages under her belt.

Condi's social life during her doctoral studies also soared to new heights. She was living her dreams with her fiancé, a professional football player. Accompanying the relationship were Denver Bronco games and get-togethers with National Football League (NFL) insiders. Behind the sports veneer, Condi's childhood promise to marry a grid-iron player moved forward. Together with her mother, detailed marriage plans were underway when the relationship faded and the highly anticipated event was mutually called off. Today when talking marriage, she jokes that God has not yet sent her someone she can live with.

In contrast, her love of everything Russian was as powerful as ever and the center of her life. Condi delivered her doctoral thesis on Soviet dominion in Korbel's Balkan state entitled, *The Case of Czechoslovakia*, earning her a seat at the graduation ceremony on August 14, 1981 outdoors on the Margery Reed Quadrangle. Her next stop in pursuit of all things Russian would be Stanford University in California.

5

Nothing Less Than the Best

> "It was an exciting time. You could go to bed one night and wake up with some country having changed its social system overnight, with a new democracy to deal with."
>
> —Condoleezza Rice, from Feliz,
> *Condi: The Condoleezza Rice Story*

Condoleezza won a fellowship to the only institute in the country that could direct her passion for Soviet affairs into the practical application of national security. The Stanford Center of International Security and Arms Control was foremost in turning out government arms control policymakers. She quickly immersed herself into campus life among the university's eight thousand picturesque acres set against the cool waters of San Francisco Bay in Palo Alto.

Away from her parents for only the second time in her life, she pursued her favorite topic in debates expressed

Assistant professor Condoleezza Rice at Stanford University. In 1981, Rice became a fellow at Stanford University's arms control and disarmament program.

with charming, opinionated, zestful intelligence and in research with methodical graceful logic that could not be missed by Professor Coit Blacker and others in the political science department. They quickly saw that this incredible black woman dovetailed beautifully with their affirmative action goals. What started as a one-year, thirty thousand-dollar fellow, had evolved into an assistant professorship by the fall semester . Affirmative action got her in the door through which she would have had to exit in three years, had she not demonstrated her capabilities in the new teaching position. The department had enough Soviet experts. Condi's courses therefore, needed to extend beyond her favorite subject. She always enjoyed a good challenge, particularly one for which she was well equipped. So the twenty-six-year-old tackled her research fellowship and teaching responsibilities with an infectious zeal and the common man clarity that Josef Korbel always demanded.

She enthusiastically laid before her students the inescapable applications of political science in current international alliances, military and weapons strategies, and economic influences. The courses she taught were ultimately about power—how it operates and how it is used. Believing that text work alone did not adequately convey the complexity of such power, she adopted role-playing methods that required her students' total involvement in recreating the birth of major foreign policies. Students researched and wrote papers on assigned projects, which could entail breaking news. Having assimilated the fundamental information surrounding policy decisions, they spent a week reenacting events.

By physically and emotionally delving inside the teeming political atmosphere from all viewpoints, roles from bureaucrats and media to lobbyists and consumerists sometimes became so intense that participants were stunned at their own improvisations. "It's interesting to watch students come to terms with how they behave," Condi observed. "They will say, 'I never thought I could behave that way.'" Political role-playing was a powerful tool. Being an oral learner, Condi recognized the lasting impression interactive recreations could have in a group setting.

Another method Condi used to maneuver impressionable minds through complex political realities was the liberal use of analogies. Football analogies, especially, were her way of getting to the crux of territorial conquests between nations. She continued to employ this technique with equal success in the White House. Coming from an educational background highly stocked in personal attention, Condi topped her classwork with as much one-on-one feedback as time would allow. At the end of the three-year period her collective approaches of engaging students and stimulating their curiosity resulted in more than the renewal of her assistant professorship. It triggered the bestowal of the Walter J. Gores Award for Excellence in Teaching, the school's highest honor.

Anyone, who had assumed that Condi was simply a statistical fit for the school's affirmative action policy, certainly was proven wrong in her first few years at Stanford. Condi was far more complicated than that. In this white, male-dominated enclave, Condi built a comfortable life where she could be herself—a Republican in liberal Democratic environs, a deeply religious person in the midst of highly analytical thinking, and a self-proclaimed black woman with a yen for shopping. As for satisfying romance, she plunged into the dating scene, and, in her free time, she quite naturally always made time for sports.

MAKING OPPORTUNITIES

She became just as active in extracurricular functions in the Palo Alto community as on campus grounds. A chance encounter with the pastor of an African American Baptist Church at Lucky's Supermarket drew her back to Sunday services playing piano for his congregation in 1981. To satisfy her soul, she returned to her roots about six months later when she joined Menlo Park Presbyterian Church. While on campus in 1982 she became involved in

Condoleezza Rice won the Walter J. Gores Award for Excellence in Teaching in 1984. Appearing from left to right: Teaching Assistant Naushad Forbes, Assistant Professor Rice, and Professor Sanford M. Dornbusch.

the school administrative activities of the Undergraduate Admissions and Financial Aid committee, the same year her mother received her Master of Arts degree.

The 1980s—1984, to be exact—also marked the publication of Condi's first book, *Uncertain Allegiance, The Soviet Union and the Czechoslovak Army 1948-1963*. Her friend Professor Coit Blacker introduced Condi to Gary Hart who was duly impressed and, despite her Republican status, coopted her aboard his brief Democratic presidential campaign as a foreign policy advisor.

But it would be Brent Scowcroft who diligently prepared her for a run at a government position. The two met at a dinner following his talk on arms control. Condi caught his attention when she persuasively challenged Scowcroft, then the head of the Commission on Strategic Forces in the Reagan Administration, on some conventional policies. He decided to monitor her class lecture on the MX missile. Impressed with her confidence and wisdom, Scowcroft began inviting her to seminars and conferences where Condi would meet the "movers and shakers" of foreign and military policy. Scowcroft's mentoring made Rice a familiar name and face among people who could pave her way to a political career in Washington, D.C.

Condi hit another pinnacle with receipt of a National Fellowship from the Hoover Institution on War, Revolution, and Peace. The fellowship allowed her the opportunity to work full time researching a second book, *The Gorbachev Era*, coauthored with the distinguished Soviet scholar Alexander Dallin. No sooner was she riding high on further exploration of Russian political relations when she was shaken to the core by her mother's death from breast cancer. She told *Essence* magazine in 2002 that her mother's death was the one regret she has, "She was only 61 when she died. But I'm grateful that she lived until I was 30. She first had breast cancer when I was 15, so she lived quite a long time." Often viewed as an independent woman of steel, the true Condi relied on her faith in God, music, family, and friends to get her past the emotional turmoil that her mother's death brought about. Accepting what could not be changed, Condi would now have to set her own anchor on her remaining sail through life.

Her second book was published by the Stanford Alumni Press in 1986. That same year her stature in the academic community heightened a notch. She joined the Board of Directors of the Stanford Mid-Peninsula Urban Coalition. Much like her father, Condi had an abiding concern for the welfare and economic development of minorities in the United States. The Urban Coalition gave her a chance to act on those concerns. When Condi's Hoover Fellowship came to a successful conclusion, her former professor George Brinkley helped her receive a Council on Foreign Relations fellowship, which pulled her into nuclear strategic planning for the Joint Chiefs of Staff in Washington, D.C. She was appointed special assistant to the Director of the Joint Chiefs of Staff at the Pentagon. Clustered in an office with three other workers, the experience elevated her respect for military officers, and apparently impressed decision-makers at Stanford.

Upon her return to the university in 1987, Condi received a tenured promotion to associate professor of political science, and added public speaking engagements to an already packed schedule. She also joined the university's Public Service Center Steering Committee and later made an administrative commitment to the Executive Committee of the Institute for International Studies. Given her broad popularity within Stanford's academic community, it's not surprising that she would be awarded a director position in the graduate studies department, and a membership on the Faculty Senate. As a trustee on the Carnegie Endowment for International Peace board, she maintained sporadic involvement in U.S./Soviet relations.

PRESENT AT THE TRANSITION

Condi's short-term forays into government policies came to a boil in February 1989. Newly appointed National Security Advisor (NSA) Brent Scowcroft cajoled her into directing the office of Soviet and East European Affairs in the NSC. Her decision to take a leave of absence from Stanford was rewarded, subsequently, with the expanded role of special assistant to the president for national security affairs and a promotion to senior director. When brought into the sphere of President George H. Bush and First Lady Barbara Bush, she found ready friends. The president wanted the individuals he needed and trusted most by his side. Brent Scowcroft was one of those people and Condoleezza Rice became another during an incredible period in history.

Downward economic pressures had finally overtaken the Soviet Union's military expansion. The country's president, Mikhail Gorbachev, embarked on a course pushing aside Cold War business as usual for a warmer relationship with the United States. Rice was part of a select delegation at the Malta Summit where Bush first met Gorbachev. President Bush introduced Condi saying, "This is Condoleezza Rice. She tells me everything I know about the Soviet Union." A quizzical Gorbachev gazed at the youthful specialist and remarked, "I hope she knows a lot." Gorbachev came to respect Condi's knowledge over the years. A genuine friendship emerged from their encounter and persisted long after he stepped down from the Russian presidency.

But in the early days of their relationship, Rice's responsibilities consisted of working with a team of special advisors to assemble and analyze information highlighting critical military, economic, and political issues, and finding ways to resolve those sensitive international situations. Some looming questions were—what new relationship should be built between the former military rivals? Should the United States stand down its weapons? Should the United States encourage freedom for surrounding East

European states trying to wrestle away from Russia's grip? Rice's briefing papers were coupled with contingency plans if the resolutions did not follow their prescribed course. Findings typically were submitted in written summaries to be used by the NSC, as well as the president. Thus, amid the swirling storm on U.S. and Soviet ships in the Mediterranean Sea, the group hammered out the makings of détente and mutual cooperation.

Condi came into her own at the NSC by growing into an indispensable part of European diplomacy. Earlier that year she was a member of Bush's advisory team in Poland during his meeting with Lech Walesa of the Solidarity Party and General Wojciech Jaruzelski of the Polish government, in the country's bid for independence from the USSR. Rice proved early on that she was the "real thing." For example, on one occasion at the White House, her NSC role required showing Russian diplomat Boris Yeltsin her hard edge to keep him in line. Their initial meeting occurred before Yeltsin's political faction had ousted Gorbachev. At that point, the blustering Yeltsin only qualified for a meeting with National Security Advisor Brent Scowcroft to which the president would drop by for an introduction. Yeltsin, incensed by what he thought was a breach of protocol, demanded to be taken to the Oval Office. Condi felt it best to assume a hard line with recalcitrant Russians. She cordially greeted him at his car for her assignment to escort him to Scowcroft. When Yeltsin refused, she met his five-minute glare with her own piercing gaze, then confidently stated she would advise General Scowcroft that Yeltsin chose not to attend the meeting. She had surprised Yeltsin, the forthcoming Russian president, by coolly agreeing with his bluff to return to the hotel. But rather than be dismissed from the White House driveway, he permitted Condi to lead him to the National Security Advisor.

It was at the historic Malta Summit that Rice truly saw how the Soviets operated in the worldwide arena. Gorbachev held out for a slow reunification of Germany, but Condi believed that five years would leave too much time for Soviet countermeasures to thwart East Germany's progress to free itself from Russia. The president heeded her call for an expeditious union of East and West Germany. The two German entities signed a treaty in October 1990, agreeing to fast-track unification. To everyone's surprise a relatively bloodless Russian coup took place the next year, and the Soviet Union of the Cold War era ceased to exist. In due time, Baltic states also fell away from Russian control like a line of dominos. President Yeltsin raised the white, blue, and red flag of the new Russian Federation over the economically strapped Kremlin. Until she left the senior director of Soviet and East European Affairs spot, Condi was front and center in shaping European policy for this new world order.

The period after the Soviet crisis felt anticlimactic to Rice. She recalled that the exhilaration of her first occasion in the Oval Office was amazing. "I remember my first Oval Office meeting; an ambassador had come to report to the President. I was completely overwhelmed by the Oval." She continued her revelry, "But after a while the ether wears off. I remember coming back from a trip to Moscow in September 1990. It was Saturday afternoon, and there was a message that Brent Scowcroft wanted me to call him. He said, 'Can you come to the White House? We're going to meet Gorbachev on Friday in Finland to talk about the Gulf War.' And I said to myself, Another meeting! Then I thought, Listen to you! When you started this job, you would have given your right arm to meet with Gorbachev, and now all of a sudden, it's another meeting with Gorbachev. So it does begin to wear off. But you should never let it wear completely off, because it's a special privilege to do this."

BROADENED BY EXPERIENCE

Not long after the NSC bloom started to fade, Pete Wilson vacated his Senate seat for a stint in the California governor's mansion. The *New Yorker*, using Brent Scowcroft as their source, reported that President Bush recommended Rice for the open Senate seat. Wilson did not confirm such a conversation with the elder Bush, but did say that Rice's name was on his list for serious consideration. Thinking of herself as an academic, Rice opted to remain at her NSC post until returning to her professorial routine at Stanford. Above all she longed for a fuller life that demanded less than a six-day, ninety-hour workweek; but the gameboard is never the same after breaking bread with presidents and sculpting a new day in history.

Sure she returned to the fun of shopping in malls for shoes and clothes, the relaxation of playing the piano, dating athletes and businessmen, exercising to Led Zepplin, and lounging in front of the television for marathon football; but her proximity to global transformation had expanded her reach considerably. It gave her the basis for a new class and a third book, *Germany Unified and Europe Transformed: A Study in Statecraft* with Philip Zelikow, a colleague during the transformation. It gave her the taste for more leadership responsibilities. Getting back into college administration issues, she chaired the Graduate Admissions Committee for a year. While Condi was not interested in Governor Wilson's Senate seat, she stuck her hand into state politics by joining his advisory panel for redistricting California. Essentially the panel contributed guidance to redrawing voter boundaries for the state assembly and senate congressional districts.

In 1991, Condi also accepted the senior fellow position at the Hoover Institute where she became acquainted with another Hoover fellow, George Schultz. Schultz opened the boardroom doors of Chevron oil company to her, and appointments to the boards of Transamerica and Hewlett-Packard Corporation soon followed. In concert with promotions and elevated government experience, the list of board memberships grew proportionately with her career, solidifying her financial future with generous cash and stock compensation packages. Schultz, a former secretary of state, also held a certain amount of sway in high government places to augment Brent Scowcroft's mentoring in that area.

Once a summer intern at RAND, Condi returned to join Brent Scowcroft in the boardroom of an expanded RAND organization that encompassed education, healthcare, international economics, and other issues of national interest. Board membership was another way to have a direct impact on the arts she so adored. For one term, she graced the board of the National Endowment for the Humanities which supplied federal grants to promote cultural enrichment.

She tapped into some of the most prestigious foreign policy groups in America. The nonpartisan Aspen Strategy Group, led by Scowcroft, headed the list. In spite of the added responsibilities, her work with political science students continued. In May 1993, Condi earned a full professorship at Stanford. A month later University President Gerhard Casper had something much bigger in mind for her.

6

Taking Control

"It's funny that I would choose that time at Stanford [as her greatest achievement]. I think it's because that was probably the toughest couple of years I went through. There were so many doubters."

—Condoleezza Rice, from Wilkerson,
"The Most Powerful Woman in the World,"
Essence, February 2002

Gerhard Casper, provost of the University of Chicago, sat before the Stanford selection committee as he vied for the president position at Stanford. Condi Rice participated in the 1992 search for the next president of Stanford University. Although Gerhard was the one under review, he was quickly impressed with Condi's intellectual range and eloquence. Observing her in action after assuming the presidency only deepened his regard for her.

Condoleezza Rice at Stanford University. In 1993, she became the first woman and the first African American to hold the position of provost at the university.

The following year, Rice had accomplished much; but little did she know that Stanford's president, Gerhard, would tap her for the prestigious position of university provost. Afterall, she had never administered a department, let alone a one and a half-billion-dollar budget. Condi had no idea Gerhard intended to appoint her provost at the time. There were plenty of the gray-haired, white-skinned, traditional male deans and department chairmen, who would gladly accept such a prestigious position. Nevertheless, Gerhard informed Condi that the job was hers for the taking. By appointing Rice, Gerhard had selected the youngest, first female, first African-American provost at Stanford.

After factoring her Republican leanings into the atypical appointment, it is not hard to imagine the controversy following the announcement of the new provost. Gerhard admitted race and gender played a role in his decision, but the university was at a juncture that required a sound decision maker who had the ability to withstand fallout from cutting an additional twenty million dollars off financial projections. Many liberal thinkers had accepted the budget deficit as a fact of university life. Condi, on the other hand, did not view balancing any budget as an impossible dream. She established it as a two-year objective, then dispassionately slashed departments and instituted policy decisions that were immediately felt by fourteen hundred faculty members.

Early on, young female and minority supporters expected Condi to be the long awaited representative of their diverse causes. They were greatly disappointed with her rejection of numerous proposals and some cuts in their ranks—so much so their complaints of bias spawned yet another federal investigation, this time by the Department of Labor. Condi, nevertheless, stood firm in her march toward fiscal stability. Her logic became clear in later research on employee diversity.

MAKING THE TOUGH DECISION

During her formal acceptance of the rocky road ahead, she stated, "Just as I was fortunate to be given a chance to help shape America's response to the extraordinary events that ended the Cold War, I am honored President Casper [Gerhard] has placed faith in my judgment and ability to meet Stanford's challenges." More importantly she had confidence in her own capabilities to reshape the face of the university in a rationale manner that served the best interest of the school. "When I decided to return to the university two years ago," she told the crowd at her induction, "I did so with even greater commitment to and appreciation of the freedom of thought, exploration and expression that the academy allows." She explained, "There is no other environment that can match the energy of a place like this."

Condi's involvement in university committees had made her intimately familiar with the inner workings of the school and her crash study of the budget process tuned up her financial skills. But whether or not that helped her anticipate all the issues crossing her desk, she did exhibit the competency to manage the institution out of its greatest problems. In doing so, she demonstrated an openness to discuss the broad spectrum of viewpoints blowing over campus grounds. For Condi had always lectured her students, "If you find yourself in the company of people who agree with you, you're in the wrong company." Well, she experienced no problem on that front. The university was populated with many vocal opponents to her policies. Although willing to listen, Condi would not be held back by endless debate or managed by irreconcilable committees. Consistent with her vision of power flowing from the top, she held her own counsel and doled out the yeas and nays necessary to sweep away the budget deficit within three years. She concurrently racked up a fourteen million dollar reserve from well-invested endowments and successful fund raising.

Condi recognized that fiscal recovery did not emerge solely from budget reductions, but, rather, by creating an attractive atmosphere that benefactors could be persuaded to preserve and with which people wanted to affiliate. To this end, President Gerhard, a faculty team, and Rice sought to create richly personal experiences for undergraduate students. Integral to the Stanford undergraduate experience would be small group courses and more research-oriented opportunities for students. Another change to her credit involved the university's core humanities requirement. Standing in stark contrast to expected Western thinking, Condi successfully spearheaded the integration of African and European history, saying Africans and Europeans arrived in America together and built the country together.

Less progress was made in other areas of diversity. Unfortunately hampered by the limited one to two percent turnover in tenured faculty, female and minority representation in staffing came too gradually for some people. Condi ingeniously found new monies to sponsor additional positions for outstanding women to slowly diversify the teaching and administrative face of the university in a way more fully reflecting the changing student body.

The problems stopping at her desk as provost were widespread; but not many evoked as much ardor as that of housing. In 1998, this hot topic sparked a rally and overnight demonstration on the campus quadrangle. To offer some relief until construction could be completed, rentals were made available to graduate students at discounted rates. Condi, however, remained frustrated with the efforts of some faculty leaseholders and the surrounding community to restrict university construction. She fumed, "The notion that Stanford is some sort of irresponsible developer that will overrun the community if not checked is just peculiar to me. If you look at the fact that we've developed about one-third of this land and developed it so beautifully, if you just drive along Foothill Expressway or along Junipero Sena there is a lot of open space out there and it's because Stanford has been very responsible." In the ongoing debate, Condi left her successor with a plan to expand student housing; but because of legal shackles she foresaw a long negotiation process to fully resolve the student-faculty housing issues.

REMEMBERING THE COMMUNITY

Outside her university office, Rice took responsibility for bettering the neighboring community. Her term as provost had not distanced her contact with elementary students in the disadvantaged areas of Palo Alto. Both fiscal administration as well as her professorial duties in the political science department continued, even as the idea of a Center for the Next Generation germinated. After a dinner conversation she had with her father John and his second wife Clara, who was a principal at Menlo Oaks Middle School, they concluded sufficient education was absent in some low-income neighborhoods plagued with violence. Then they decided to do more than just talk about the problem.

John Rice had moved closer to his daughter following his retirement from the University of Denver. Spending his graying years in California after Angelena's death proved a less-than-leisurely time for Condi's Dad. Springing from an introduction by a mutual friend, he found another soul-mate in a local school principal. John and Clara married in 1989. He served on the Board of Governors of California Community Colleges. His lifetime of academic dedication was heralded with the National Alliance of Black School Educators' Living Legend Award and an honorary doctorate from Daniel Hale University in Chicago. Of course, Next Generation Center held a special place in the scheme of his life. It was causes like Next Generation that sustained the

Rice families' educational legacy, and, more specifically, gave Condi's existence greater personal meaning.

With philanthropist Susan Ford, Condi brought to life the Next Generation after-school enrichment program for children in grades three through eight. Palo Alto youngsters needed a teacher's recommendation and C+ grade average to gain access to foreign languages, the world of computers, and music offered by the program. Stanford students recruited by John pitched in with math and science for college preparatory training. Similar to John's activities in Birmingham, a qualified volunteer staff offered follow-up counseling and encouraging words for the program's one hundred to one hundred-fifty students as they progressed through high school. Next Generation opened essential doors for its students to step through and explore.

Not wanting to slight the youth organization when her university and corporate demands impinged on the program's administration, Condi merged Next Generation into the Boys and Girls Club of the Peninsula and assumed the less demanding day-to-day role of vice president in the new parent organization. Condi's concern for the future of each child in Next Generation was not in the least diminished by the reorganization.

STANFORD, THE BOARDROOM, AND LIFE IN BETWEEN

Through her many corporate positions, Condi also found time to situate her fingers deftly on the pulse of governments around the world. George Schulz mentored her into several well-respected groups, such as the International Advisory Council for J.P. Morgan, which provided exposure to high-level officials from nations south of the North American border to the Pacific Rim and across the Indian Ocean to South Africa. Her director-ships on the boards of charitable foundations at the Carnegie Corporation and nearer to home, the Hewlett-Packard Corporation, served a similar purpose, as did her government appointment to the Federal Advisory Committee on Gender in the Military.

Soon after being named provost at Stanford, she joined the Board of Trustees at her alma mater, Notre Dame, in 1994, and three years later was named that school's National Exemplar award recipient for her service to education. In 1997, her distinction in academia was further solidified by becoming one of eleven professors inducted into the American Academy of Arts and Sciences. The clamor for public appearances and a bevy of additional awards flooded her doorstep after her provost appointment.

Her days filled with work, Condi stayed grounded through music. Piano lessons from fellow professor George Barth constituted breaths of fresh air. Adding to that pleas-ure was her discovery of chamber music. She had not made it to the professional stage as originally planned, but that did not mean she had to play alone. She was invited to join a chamber music quartet of Stanford colleagues who performed for their own entertainment. Still with all their fun, the excitement of playing before a larger audience beckoned. She struck up a friendship with the touring Muir Quartet when they performed at Stanford and actually joined them once in concert on the campus stage. Condi was definitely hooked by the performance bug and returned to the Stanford footlights with her music instructor at a faculty talent show. But whether in a private group or before a concert audience, the innervating close-knit exchange among chamber musicians fit Condi's abilities to listen and collaborate like a glove. She loved it as much as playing solo.

Her exercise coach, Mark Mateska, watched Condi in an informal recital and was amazed by the physical strength classical piano required. He compared it to the exertion put forth by the team on the school football field.

Condi was not one to dwell on nostalgia. But when asked to do so, she reflected on her years at Stanford with great personal and professional satisfaction. It was a time filled with music, love, and friendship, particularly from long-term companion Gene Washington. Washington is a Stanford graduate and former star wide receiver for the San Francisco 49ers. For a while, the statuesque, five-foot eight-inch, well-toned Condi and Washington made an attractive couple. Rice's tenure at Stanford had a tangible impact on her personally in addition to the surrounding community, and elevated the university to a fiscal and academic level that few foresaw. Rice left the school as one of its most honored faculty members and administrators.

Following her successful stint as provost at Stanford, Condi developed a growing desire for new conquests. She had been informally advising George W. Bush on foreign affairs since 1998 in preparation for his presidential campaign. That endeavor stirred up her love of international politics and the travel it entailed, especially trips to Russia. Finally she decided to take another leave of absence from the university to re-explore the international arena, but with a business twist. Her plan was to gain research experience in the economic and institutional impact of globalization.

Once her decision to leave Stanford was announced, farewell parties abounded. Perhaps the most poignant gathering was with approximately one hundred African Americans in the Stanford community where the lilting strains of her favorite spirituals, "His Eyes is on the Sparrow" and "I Need Thee Every Hour," moved everyone to tears. She walked away from the Office of Provost with outstanding lessons learned and a cherished Russian first edition of Tolstoy's *War and Peace* given collectively by her Stanford friends. She had left her former job, but not the school's campus.

Condi returned to the Hoover Institute as a senior fellow.

With all that has occurred since her departure on July 1, 1999, it is surprising that she viewed her accomplishments during those tumultuous years in the provost office as her greatest achievement. But if she had to do it all over again, her friend and confidant Coit Blacker quoted her as saying she might approach the situation with a gentler hand. Then again, Condi does not spend much time contemplating the past because she is too busy focusing on the future. In this case, a future she thought would be centered around research in the Hoover Institute. Life had something else in store for her.

7

Forming a Presidency

> "I think that you will see in the presidency of George W. Bush recognition of how important it is that we continue the last 30-plus years of progress toward one America; that he will have an administration that is inclusive, an administration that is bipartisan, and perhaps most importantly, an administration that affirms that united we stand and divided we fall, and I'm very proud to have a chance to be part of it."
>
> —Condoleezza Rice, from Feliz, *Condi: The Condoleezza Rice Story*

"I've respected him from the first time we talked, because he has the kind of intellect that goes straight to the point," Condi says of her friend George W. Bush. Although the two had met in 1995, they made one-on-one time after Condi visited with Barbara and George H. Bush in their Houston home. Condoleezza believed that staying in touch served to strengthen any relationship. On that particular visit, the senior Bush suggested Condi take an excursion to reconnect with his son, Texas's latest governor, in the capital city of Austin.

Condi and Governor George W. Bush formed a lasting bond of loyalty and mutual respect at that meeting. Initially sharing their sports fanaticism, George W. gave Condi a tour of his baseball collection and shared stories with her about the Texas Rangers team that he co-owned. Condi kept pace with distinctive tales of a teenage Willie Mays in her mother's high school classes in Birmingham. The two also found common ground in their calm, genuine approach to life, not to mention their wicked sense of humor.

Condi's visits to the senior Bushes increased during 1997 as she assisted George H. Bush and Brent Scowcroft in writing *A World Transformed*, a book published in 1998, covering the monumental international political upheavals during the first Bush presidency. Rice narrated the audio version. The book trio met extensively in Houston and at Bush's summerhouse in Kennebunkport, Maine. Condi's trips to the Bush summerhouse continued after the text's completion. During one of those short vacations in 1998, George W. was entertaining thoughts of running for president and asked Condi for a review of current international issues. They chatted on the treadmill, hit a few tennis balls, and fished their way through the annals of neo-global politics. More accurately, the two Georges fished while Condi watched and talked.

George W. was not one to read weighty documents about international policies and complicated relationships. He preferred oral interpretations with recommendations that highlighted actionable options concisely and quickly. Condi had made practical easy-to-follow discussions her forte in academia. Known for being imminently approachable, her male friends and mentors often praised her non-intimidating style. Rather than flaunt her brilliance, Condi's approachability allowed others to adopt her knowledge as their own, not quite knowing where their ideas began and hers left off. She, in this patented approach, dispensed the exact blend of down-to-earth, conservative international strategies with the fun-loving humor that George W. needed. He asked her to head his foreign policy team as he hit the campaign trail in 1999.

Supporting a political campaign was not what Condi had in mind when she stepped down from the provost office, but loyalty to the friend she adores won out. She agreed to help coach him on foreign matters and lead the strategy team of Richard Armitage, Robert Zoellick, Paul Wolfowitz, Robert Blackwell, and Richard Perle; a tight-knit group she named the Vulcans. Settling on the group's title was an opportunity to compete with George W.'s penchant for quirky nicknames. Vulcan held dual significance as the Roman god of thunder and forger of metal tools for the gods, as well as the skimpily draped statue standing atop the mountain overlooking Birmingham. The green and red colors of the statue's torch alternately signal a decent traffic day or the occurrence of a fatal accident in the city. The campaign's Vulcans were almost as familiar to Condi as the Birmingham sculpture, since they were members of the senior Bush's administration. Likewise, vice presidential running mate Dick Cheney, who added to the Vulcan's stratagems, was a former chief of staff in the Ford administration and former secretary of defense for the elder Bush.

Condi entered the campaign anticipating a part-time need for her services to prepare George W. for questions on foreign affairs and to offer advice on a cursory international policy that would satisfy campaign speeches. She believed the job might also draw her into a speech or two, but for the most part she expected to remain in the background. Deborah Carson, a friend with direct experience on the Clinton campaign, predicted a more demanding scenario. Because of Condi's broad capabilities and facile brainpower, she frequently contributed to committees and situations well outside her specialty of foreign affairs. The whirlwind of Bush's political campaign proved no different.

Political opponents played up Bush's inexperience in international affairs, questioned his commitment to minorities and women, and even raised concerns about his intellectual capacity for the office of U.S. president. More and more Bush relied upon his trusted friend, Condi, to coach him through those highly publicized issues and any others that arose during the campaign. Even with written talking points, George W. preferred lengthy, intense question and answer sessions to meld the necessary discussion points with their accompanying background. He wanted Condi by his side to manage that process during and between public appearances. By virtue of her race and gender, Condi also was an obvious choice to present Bush's speeches, deflecting perceptions of Bush's indifference to minorities. She also served in the "W is for Women" countermeasures with the Bush wives and Lynne Cheney, wife of the running mate.

Staying on top of all those fires required Condi to join the bandwagon full time crisscrossing the United States and rapidly digesting a host of domestic, economic, and non-European international facts along the way. Her one sure break from politics was Sunday services in church where the Bush team respected her request not to be disturbed. During other moments, the national media watched the young authoritative, Black female sophisticate velvet-gloving her way around the conservative gray-haired white Republican boys club. Condi's concern was not in becoming a media darling or even obtaining a position in the White House. Once she became immersed in the campaign full time, she thought no further than getting her candidate an election majority. That in itself was no easy feat.

GETTING THE VOTE

Public sentiment between Bush and his Democratic opponent, then-incumbent Vice President Al Gore, ran neck and neck. Gore battled the media wash from the series of scandals that dogged President Bill Clinton. Insinuations that Gore lacked truthfulness and a homey star quality added more fuel to the fire. On the other side of the battle, Bush's camp had its own set of image problems, including questions about his intelligence and acumen for international diplomacy. Beyond those issues, his conservative stance on affirmative action repelled many minorities, while his support of the right wing pro-lifers in the party caused an irreparable split with Republicans who advocated that women should be free to choose with regard to birth control.

Such circumstances made the new millennium image of a Republican Party that is inclusive and bipartisan all the more important. Condi helped hammer out those concepts and assisted the big push for them at

Condoleezza Rice addresses the Republican National Convention in Philadelphia on August 1, 2000. Speaking about the Republican Party, Rice said, "I found a party that sees me as an individual, not as part of a group."

the 2000 Republican Convention in Philadelphia, Pennsylvania. Taking the stage to speak about her membership in the Republican Party, she explained, "I found a party that sees me as an individual, not as part of a group. I found a party that puts family first. I found a party that believes that peace begins with strength."

She continued, "George W. Bush and Dick Cheney live and breathe these Republican principles. They understand what is required for our time and what is timeless."

With Condi's assistance, Bush promoted the notion of a stronger independent America; one that would not act as a global policeman following the lead of the United Nations. He depicted an organized America coordinating worldwide relations with less intercession in the Palestinian-Israeli conflict and complex Middle East issues. He described a fit, stream-lined United States government focused on its own national interests in the Western Hemisphere closer to home. To that end, he planned a reduction of military forces in places such as the Balkans and Persian Gulf in favor of redeployment closer to the United States, perhaps in Central and South America.

Since her time at Notre Dame, Condi has held a strong nationalist approach to global politics. In her research she observed that every country, whether during times of peace or periods of aggression, act in their best interest. To her, following the normal order by holding American needs first is a logical approach when developing international strategies. And, what better time to act unilaterally than in the absence of the former Cold War rivalry with the Soviet Union? The United States emerged from that showdown as the strongest sovereignty in the world, eminently capable of determining where and how its strength should be applied.

Condi and George W. share a common perspective about wielding executive power without the endless red tape of international policymaking organizations. Condi certainly is willing to listen to any country's opinion or discourse that makes sense to America, but inconsistent aimless diatribes likely will be cut short. She also believes strong governance does not conflict with a deep-rooted faith in God and political ethics, because serving the best interest of its people and accompanying morals are at the heart of any great nation. On those matters George W. and Condi also agree. More recently Rice stated when it comes to decisions, "I know that the President [George W. Bush] is always going to ask first what is the principled thing to do or the right thing to do."

George W. won the privilege to rule from the executive chair in the Oval Office for one presidential term. Bush gained the seat in a history-making battle that took both Republican and Democratic parties to the Supreme Court for justice. Due to irregularities, Democrats demanded a recount of certain voting districts in Florida, the state governed by Bush's brother. Debates also raged about absentee ballots. Tight election results nationally, which gave Gore the edge on the popular vote and Bush the electoral college, forced officials in the pivotal state of Florida to tally hanging chads, the tiny residual circle remaining from a partially punched paper ballot. The victory for Bush took weeks to sort out and garnered media scrutiny from around the world. It certainly proved one fascinating election for the record books.

While legal papers continued to be exchanged between Democratic and Republican parties in an effort to resolve the conflict, Bush donned the mantel of President-elect and began building his cabinet and key advisors. The Supreme Court ruling against the Democrats eventually sealed his election. Similar to his father with Brent Scowcroft, George W. chose to keep a most trusted individual by his side. At a press conference on December 18, 2000, he announced three appointments, National Security Advisor Condoleezza Rice, White House Counsel Al Gonzales, and Counselor to the President Karen Hughes. Of the three, Condi would remain beside him whenever he traveled and have constant access to the Oval Office. To the press Bush said, "Dr. Rice is not only a brilliant person, she is an experienced person. She is a good manager. I trust her judgment. Americans will find that she is a wise person, and I'm so honored [she is] joining the administration." Fortunately, Condi's father survived a heart attack long enough to hear the announcement. He was both delighted in her success and sad that it would take her away from California. Since his death she has gained national attention, but in the absence of her father, she feels like nobody's little girl.

Having faith that her parents were together in heaven, Rice immediately turned to business in her West-Wing office, just down the hall from the commander-in-chief. In selecting her, Bush knew that he could confide in Condi, and that she would be an honest broker in distilling the myriad of opinions sliding through his door into discernible policy. By accepting the position, Condi had to resign from her lucrative spot on the Chevron board, which was soon followed by the removal of her name from one of the company's supertankers. She did not, however, sever her ties entirely with Stanford University.

Although she purchased an apartment in the Watergate complex in the Georgetown/Foggy Bottom section of Washington and furnished it with cherished mementos, Rice has retained her condo on Stanford's campus. After all, there is life after Washington.

8

Team Player

> "All agencies are stakeholders and each has a role in the solution. But it is also true that we can't have as many solutions as there are federal agencies. We have to coordinate among the government's naturally occurring stovepipes. We have to encourage common standards."
>
> —Condoleezza Rice, U.S. Chamber of Commerce, The White House Office of the Press Secretary, March 2001

Past National Security Councils were often embroiled in turf wars between the Department of State and the bailiwicks of other cabinet members. George W. made it clear he did not want to preside over such public squabbles. He was relying on his cabinet and ancillary advisors to operate like a well-trained team. Their working relationship was undoubtedly helped by the fact that many of the advisors

National Security Advisor Rice talks with Secretary of State Colin Powell while attending a 2001 meeting between President George W. Bush and Spanish Prime Minister Jose Maria Aznar. Rice and Powell worked together to help form the Bush administration's international policy.

served together in previous administrations. Condi, for example, became a fixture at Colin Powell's house during her prior stint in Washington. She and his wife Alma Powell already shared an upscale Birmingham history. Colin became so comfortable with the young woman that when she arrived at their door he would announce "Condi's home" to Alma. Not even Vice President Cheney, the former Secretary of Defense for the senior Bush, building what appeared to be a mini-NSC in his office, could distract

Condi from her task to support the president in devising foreign strategies and the Council in formulating related policies using collaborative processes.

She further resolved that her organization would not cross into the area of implementing foreign policies or public communication that bred much of her predecessor's infighting. Condi saw no need to engage in policy implementation and intelligence gathering. Nevertheless, the NSC does keep the president informed with regard to strategic direction. Condi's job entails preparing George W. for diplomatic meetings and public appearances. She also remains by his side throughout most presidential trips, or sends her deputy on shorter junkets.

Condi is the first woman to perform this advisory function, and follows in the footsteps of her friends Brent Scowcroft, Colin Powell, Henry Kissinger, and Zbigniew Brzezinski. She is not likely to admit to gender differences in her approach to the job. She does say, "I'm pretty good at bringing people together, even strong personalities together… But, it is important, when you've got strong personalities and strong egos, to try and get people on the same page and that's what I do for a living." She likes to find some point of consensus to begin NSC meetings with the president prior to delving into disparate opinions. Between those meetings, Condi takes the president's basic direction and works with the various personalities on the Council to craft supportable strategies and policies.

Regarding questions abut her robustness for the post, underestimating Condi is an old story that she pushes aside as she always has. She entered the job with knowledge of global issues, and when more information is needed she has cadres of experienced advisors and specialists at her disposal. Just as one of her predecessors, Brent Scowcroft, called her for advice during the Gulf War, Condi draws upon others outside the NSC who have walked in lofty diplomatic and military shoes.

She has served under two Bush presidents who both know, when she has a job, it will be done objectively and with excellence. Condi likewise knows she belongs in her White House office and earned her place there as predicted when she was ten years old. "My family is third-generation college-educated. I should've gotten to where I am," she told the *Washington Post*. There was no reason for her to be uncomfortable about possibly having more familiarity with the upstairs presidential residence than other advisors. The trust of the president and his family too has been earned.

Using her observations and personal experiences as the basis, Rice describes herself as quite conservative on foreign policy and gun control, much like George W., but more libertarian to moderate on other issues. If her widespread policy views diverged from the president's overall conservative perspective, the public has not heard about it. Only on one point did she seem to openly, but cautiously deviate from the party line. That has been the steady Republican opposition to affirmative action and statements about the existence of a level playing field. Somehow, even for this controversial issue, she and Bush managed to find a centerpoint that both could present publicly—racism still exists but affirmative action quotas are unnecessary.

INSIDE THE NSC

George W. and his national security advisor understood each other perfectly. They did not need a signed directive outlining the structure of the NSC as the last two administrations had. The Council design was inherent in Bush's campaign promises and international strategies. Armed with her working papers, Condi hit the ground running. The first few weeks required restructuring her staff to align with the president's slant on foreign policy. Russia did not carry the power and antagonism it once had against America. Its current standing, therefore, could not justify analyzing its every move on the globe or filtering the foreign policy for all other nations through a Russian lens. During Condi's previous time in the NSC, memos on almost all situations around the globe passed through her office for her signature of concurrence because of potential Soviet interests worldwide. Those days are no more. Russian and East European offices are consolidated with the rest of Europe consistent with handling Russia the same as any strong European ally.

Other offices monitoring various global relationships were also realigned according to George W. and Condi's joint worldview. The Southeast Asia watch returned to the Asia sector. North Africa was shifted to the Near East where most Arab nations fell. The rest of Africa was assigned to a separate unit, so too the rest of the Western Hemisphere.

This was going to be the new information age presidency that factored economics into its foreign policy. That is why Treasury Secretary Paul O'Neill and an economic department were added to the team. It also was time for a leaner organization. The inherited Clinton format of more than one hundred staffers was reduced by one-third. Condi eliminated group operations that fell under other White House or cabinet departments and/or had lower priority on the president's decision-making hierarchy. Environmental and health units were disbanded within the

NSC and those issues were left to their respective federal organizations. Redundancies with the main White House staff in communications and legislative responsibilities were likewise removed.

The Nonproliferation and Export Controls Office became focused solely on defense in the new Counter-Proliferation and Homeland Defense Office, which advocated a national missile defense system, a reduction in excess nuclear warheads, and an increase in conventional hi-tech armaments. No significant changes were made to the Office for Transnational Threats left from the Clinton years under Richard A. Clarke.

At the start of George W.'s administration there was a lot of ground to cover. There was the issue of getting the North Atlantic Treaty Organization (NATO) to recognize the new European order and to adopt Balkin flashpoints into its plain of military coverage. Condi has been concerned that when it comes to such eastern sectors, NATO has offered too little assistance, leaving the United States to fill the gap policing the most volatile European countries.

Within her offices due attention is given to the Strategic Arms Limitation Treaty (SALT) and Anti-Ballistic Missile Treaty (ABM) with the Russians, which Condi believes are Cold War relics that serve to limit George W.'s future defense strategy. The Russian-U.S. nuclear arms race that SALT II and ABM treaties largely controlled is essentially dead and buried. Condi and the president feel that the United States should pursue defense on the basis of its own interests without Russian constraints. The administration did agree to further reduce its number of nuclear warheads and agreed with the concept of Russia monitoring the testing of new defenses, most notably the space-based "Star Wars" missile defense shield that Russia opposes.

George W. also gave substantial attention to U.S. trade interests particularly interests in Asia and the economic minefields of Central and South America. Argentina, for example, was promised continued United States support if its zero-deficit plan was pursued and it worked with the International Monetary Fund to restructure a mounting national debt. Through it all, Condi was content to travel by the president's side, but remain in the background. She has no need to step into the "spotlight," having cemented her relationship with the president as a trusted colleague and key advisor.

PRE-9/11

Before the terrorist attacks of 9/11, some people wondered if Condi was over her head in this high-level position. After 9/11 many questions persisted. For example, some wondered if her intelligence analysis had failed? After all, her office provides the main forum from which the president considers national security and foreign policy matters. Condi's pivotal role of preparing NSC principals for regular bi-weekly meetings chaired by the president, as well as presenting analyses, and preparing summaries of the group's opinions and data to the president made her a lightning rod for public criticism in the wake of the 9/11 attacks.

She used her total access to the president to keep him informed of critical issues, to assist him in formulating his strategies, and to keep him abreast of global shifts that could affect his policies. The increase in intelligence traffic regarding terrorist activities while Bush was forming his administration is a case in point. Condi received an extensive briefing on terrorism during the presidential transition, a period when threats were on the rise. By the time the Bush team was securely in their offices between April–May 2001, possible al Qaida stikes against U.S. targets and interests were being reported. Based on the history of terrorism and the nature of the intelligence received, the danger was interpreted to extend to United States presence in the Middle East, Arabian Peninsula, and Europe.

The month of June brought some terrorists to justice with arrests for the Millennium plot (thought to be unrelated to al Qaida). Testimony by participants in that plan suggested there might be interest in attacking the United States, but it was not clear how or where such an assault would occur. Although nonspecific, spikes in terrorist threats during that period drew enough concern for the Federal Aviation Administration (FAA) to issue an information circular to private carriers through law enforcement. The State Department also issued a world-wide caution, and NSC Special Assistant Dick Clark called a meeting of the inter-agency Counterterrorism Security Group to address the proliferating reports of possible terrorist activity.

FBI messages in early July seemed to confirm overseas danger. While the FBI could not confirm or foresee any specific domestic attacks, they felt that such attacks could not be ruled out. At least one of the threats specifically suggested the use of explosives in an unknown airport terminal by associates of the Millennium plot. The sheer volume of threats became substantial enough for the president to ask Condi for a briefing on the defensive actions being taken. Her Counterterrorism Security Group was already in the process of bringing domestic agencies on board for deeper analyses. The group's concern rose about potential strikes in Paris, Turkey, and Rome leading them to suspend nonessential travel of their U.S. staff and to meet almost daily either fully or in subgroups to build contingency plans for multiple and simultaneous attacks around the world.

In mid-July, much of the increased intelligence warned of possible danger at the upcoming G8 summit of super-power nations in Italy, and the CIA went on full alert to contain potential terrorism. Their diligence thwarted attacks in the three areas of highest concern in Paris, Rome, Turkey, and in Genoa, Italy, where the G8 ultimately met, unhampered by terrorism or the violent demonstrations outside their protected red zone. Yet, because of repeated overseas threats, the FAA issued another information circular urging civil aviation to use the "highest level of caution." During the month, the FBI continued to report threats related to the conviction of Millennium plot terrorists. The FAA issued another official circular at the end of July once again urging caution, but now because terrorist groups were planning and training for hijackings. It, however, stated that no specific target or credible terroristic threats to U.S. civil aviation had been identified.

The FBI issued an intelligence letter at the start of August reiterating possible threats overseas, and danger specifically related to the third anniversary of the bombings in East Africa. Soon after, the president received a briefing that included an analytical report on terrorism and the forms it had taken in recent history. Further reports prompted the FAA to pass along updates that terrorists were disguising weapons in cell phones, key chains, and pens.

Perhaps most alarming to government officials were reports naming President Bush as the target, which spear-headed caution despite the fact that the office of the president would not be shut down by general threats. Business had to go on. Behind the backdrop of the administration's full domestic and international agenda, increased reports of potential terrorism were being investigated by the NSC and collaborative agencies in hopes of narrowing the general information into more actionable terms. Unfortunately, not all pertinent conclusions and recommendations from the field made it beyond the chambers of their respective agencies.

"I think people appreciated the urgency and the threat, and I think both we and the Clinton Administration were trying to deal seriously and aggressively with al Qaida," Condi explained to Margaret Warner on *Newshour*, "but we have learned since September 11, that there was inadequate intelligence sharing for a host of traditional and cultural and in fact reasons going to the very nature of who we are about what the FBI and the CIA could share." In the absence of more specificity regarding the risks at hand, the best U.S. public and private organizations could do was stay alert.

9

No More Than
We Can Bear

> "Ambiguity has never bothered me at all. I think that
> part of it is that I'm pretty religious, and that probably
> helps to make one less fearful and more optimistic
> about what's possible."
>
> —Condoleezza Rice,
> *Stanford Report,* June 1999

Three hijacked commercial flights hit their targets on September 11, 2001, and military forces were scrambled to defend against more attacks from the air and sea. The skies over the United States were closed to private aircraft and planes already in flight were diverted to the nearest available airport. Reports flowed in of a possible attack on the president's plane, Air Force One, as it shuttled from base to base. Taking to the air in Florida, it stopped briefly at Barksdale Air Base in Louisiana. From there the president told a shocked public that steps were being taken to protect the nation, and in no uncertain terms those responsible for the day's horrific events would be brought to justice. Then he flew to the Offutt Base in Nebraska and presided over a National Security Council meeting by phone. He was accompanied by an NSC representative rather than Condi or her deputy because as fortune would have it neither thought the president's daytrip to Florida required their presence. The fortuitous decision happened to have left Condi where she could be most effective when disaster struck.

Condi, adhering to a higher level of security when a federal building has been breached, in this case the Pentagon, headed from the Situation Room to the underground operation center called the bunker, where Vice President Cheney had already been secured. Upon arrival her first telephone call went to her aunt and uncle in Birmingham to let them know she was fine. Calls followed to the heads of state in other countries. Each leader expressed condolences for the tragic loss of life. Former U.S. presidents, in whatever country they happened to have been, were brought abreast of the news and secured.

Colin Powell boarded his flight from Peru to the United States around 10:46 A.M. Defense Secretary Donald Rumsfeld called from the Pentagon bunker and also met with senior deputies on Condi's staff. Bush's plane, accompanied by three fighter jets, finally touched down at Andrews Air Base in Maryland before dusk. From there, the president boarded his helicopter, Marine One, and was escorted by a formation of helicopters over the burning Pentagon and to the relatively peaceful White House lawn by 6:45 P.M. Soon after, the president was ready to address the nation, delivering strong words to America's attackers and those who harbor terrorists. Plans were already being made for an all-out war on terrorism.

National Security Advisor Rice during a meeting just four days after the September 11, 2001 terrorist attacks. Seated across the table from right, are Vice President Dick Cheney, Attorney General John Ashcroft, an unidentified man, and White House General Council Alberto R. Gonzales.

Mere hours after the attacks on America, explosions rang out in Kabul, the capital of Afghanistan. The damage inflicted was said to be the work of the Northern Alliance, a faction of U.S.-backed rebels fighting the ruling Taliban. It raised the question of whether those who set the attacks against America in motion were among the Taliban leaders.

The first evening following 9/11, Condi, a woman for which little kept her awake at night, did not sleep well. She recalled, "I probably woke up every thirty minutes or so." It was impossible not to reprocess the tragedy. "In this job when we face a horrible crisis like September 11, you go back in your mind and think, 'Is there anything I could have done? Might I have seen this coming? Was there some way?'" Preparing a plan of action, then placing the rest in God's hands is what eases her mind. Condi truly believes that God will never let you fall too far, because he knows how much you can bear.

POST-9/11

She rested more easily as an appropriate response evolved in subsequent days. George W. had asked for a comprehensive attack on terrorism. Biweekly NSC meetings, chaired by President Bush, immediately transformed into daily morning occurrences. Afterwards Condi reassembled Council members for further discussions and information sharing to prepare their next meeting with the president. During the course of a typical day, Condi held several additional briefings with George W. and clarified issues with individual NSC members either in person or by phone. Those phone calls began at 7:15 A.M. to obtain the latest reports from Secretary of State Colin Powell and Defense Secretary Donald Rumsfeld. The administration veered toward showing flexibility in its political direction. Against its best-laid plans to reduce U.S. involvement in the Middle East, a few unidentified people in that region had forced a different reality.

The field of suspects quickly narrowed to a range of individuals with known ties to terrorist groups that have either executed or planned attacks on American assets. The list of suspects included Sheikh Omar Abdul Rahman ("the Blind Sheikh") and Osama bin Laden and his al Qaida organization. Al Qaida operated cells internationally from mobile headquarters in Afghanistan. Bin Laden, its leader, was one of the many sons of a wealthy Saudi Arabian construction magnate. The resourceful rebel leader was believed to have substantial personal funds and also to have received millions more in his cause to liberate fellow Arabs. Removing what he saw as the chokehold Israel has on Palestinians topped his list. On more than one occasion, bin Laden had openly stated that the United States in allying with Israel shares complicity in the occupation of Palestinian lands. He, therefore, declared a "holy war" against America and its "infidel" lifestyle.

By September 24, 2001, early comprehensive efforts to cripple al Qaida resulted in freezing six million dollars in the network's thirty U.S. and twenty overseas bank accounts. In conjunction with following the money trail, twenty-seven related organizations and individuals were identified. Concurrent wheels were turning to mount an offensive military action against al Qaida strongholds in Afghanistan and the Taliban government hosting them, if necessary.

On the diplomatic front, Secretary of State Colin Powell and Defense Secretary Donald Rumsfeld pulled together a coalition of about ninety countries that supported an invasion of Afghanistan with various commitments ranging from military forces to financial backing to tacit approval. Meanwhile, Pakistani intermediaries relayed terms for the Taliban's surrender of all al Qaida operatives and trainees to the United States in order to avoid war.

When the Taliban denied the existence of terrorists in their country, war became inevitable. Soon after, the usually inconspicuous Rice could be seen each week on television or at White House press conferences, advancing the administration's War on Terrorism with emphasis on al Qaida, and how the United States intended to maintain global pressure on terrorists. She repeated that the United States was showing great restraint in orchestrating diplomatic and financial efforts to bring the alleged criminals to justice.

A week prior to the military offensive, Defense Secretary Rumsfeld traveled throughout the Middle East for a final check on the continued allegiance of many Arab states. On Friday, October 4, Rumsfeld confirmed military readiness with General Richard Myers, Chairman of the Joint Chiefs of Staff, and received an affirmative response from the commander of the invasion, General Tommy Franks, that everything was in place. All they needed was presidential approval to begin. Even though war was a foregone conclusion, Condi reassured the public, "he [the president] didn't feel any rush to get into the military piece because the campaign had begun. We were making progress. The Taliban was getting more and more isolated." In many eyes, President Bush's coming decision on when to invade Afghanistan was a sober and urgent one.

President Bush and the first lady joined family and friends from Texas, who arrived for a little relaxation at Camp David, the presidential retreat in Maryland. On the eve of war, Condi recalled beepers interrupted their traditional viewing of the televised Texas-Oklahoma football game. Not all knew what was about to happen, but Karen Hughes thought "everyone was trying hard to act normal." Bush had conducted a final review of military and political status with the NSC Saturday morning when the order was given for bombing to begin the next day on General Frank's command.

Sunday morning, October 6, 2001, found the president at a previously scheduled memorial service in Emmitsburg, Maryland for firefighters killed in the line of duty (one of several he and his staff had attended since 9/11). After his return to the White House, bombs rained down on military targets in Afghanistan. The time at the White House was 12:30 P.M. Rumsfield called Condi with the news that war was underway, and she informed the president.

Condi is pragmatic about military intervention. She sees it as a necessary final solution against any nation bent on harming the United States. "I am a realist. Power matters. But there can be no absence of moral content in foreign policy and," furthermore she believes, "the American people wouldn't accept such an absence."

Her moral and humanitarian spirit clearly distinguishes between fighting forces and civilians caught in the middle of feuding governments. She is inspired by the examples of President Harry Truman and other American presidents, who looked at the totality of the battlefield and readily understood the need for aid to feed, clothe and shelter citizens stricken by war and to restore countries crippled by defeat. Sitting around the kitchen table at Camp David, First Lady Laura Bush, Karen Hughes, and Condoleezza Rice thought of a food drop to mitigate the war's impact on the Afghan people. The unfamiliarity of the offering was met with mixed reactions from the Afghans, but the installation of a new, freer government had many celebrating in the streets and spirited the return of numerous Afghan refugees.

10

Axis of Evil

> "We all live with the spectre of World War II, and we all live with the fact that the great democracies were not able to muster the will to act even when the handwriting was pretty clear on the wall that Adolf Hitler was unstoppable except by force."
> —Condoleezza Rice, from Lehmann, "Without a Doubt," The *New Yorker*, October 14 & 21, 2002

In the January 2002 State of the Union address President Bush specifically characterized North Korea, Iran, Iraq, and their "rogue" allies as the "axis of evil," arming to threaten the the peace of the world. Condi featured prominently in crafting Bush's National Security Strategy unveiled September 17, 2002 to deal with the *axis*. From a military perspective, it is reminiscent of the early days of the Cold War and the evolution of its limited warfare strategy to fight an amorphous "communist threat" from taking over the United States and potentially the

President George W. Bush at his 2002 State of the Union Address during which he called North Korea, Iran, and Iraq an "axis of evil."

world. This time terrorism has emerged as a more tangible enemy that must be deterred at enormous costs, including toppling the "rogue" governments. To that end, Congress granted the president great powers to investigate and root out terrorist threats before further damage can be done.

FIGHTING TERRORISM

Inside U.S. borders and territories a new cabinet-level Homeland Security Department was formed reporting directly to the president through its head, former Pennsylvania Governor Tom Ridge. To date, efforts mark an era of military presence or heightened law enforcement in airports and guarding the country's other sensitive infrastructure. Citizens must accept more stringent checkpoints and even searches when entering large buildings, particularly government facilities and airports. If deemed necessary, unlimited incarceration and interrogation is being used to find and shut down terrorist cells operating on U.S. soil, before they can reap destruction. Spot checks along U.S. borders and overflight patrols of U.S. skies have increased. Color-coded warnings were created to alert the public to the degree of pending threats to the nation. This entire security process means building a new cross-functional operation and reorganizing the FBI to meet the challenges of covert and highly adaptable terrorists in America. It also necessitates more coordinated data at the federal, state and local levels.

From an international perspective, as reflected by recent strategies, U.S. overseas actions will continue to liberate societies from terrorism, disarm them of weapons of mass destruction, and usher them into democracy. Then spark them into economic growth via free markets and free trade by reshaping regulatory, tax and financial policies, and rule of law. Joint international efforts also will continue to identify and detain terrorists while attacking their leadership around the globe in an effort to prevent execution of plots against U.S. assets (both people and property) or at the very least bring to justice those who perpetrate violence against the United States.

In the information age, this cloak of protection must extend well beyond coordinating military and police forces to also encompass protecting computer networks that increasingly sustain public and private operations. It entails linking data systems either physically or through some other form of information sharing for proactive use to police enemies of the state, freezing assets, tracing movements of individuals and more. This can only be accomplished with the cooperation of private entities, corporations, and individuals.

At the center of this latest terrorist firestorm lay the Palestinian–Israeli conflict. The U.S. pledges to work toward the establishment of "an independent and democratic Palestine, living beside Israel in peace and security." Where similar age-old disputes exist in Asia and Africa, America will encourage peaceful and democratic coexistence. The United States will stand against drug cartels in South America, and disease and poverty in Africa.

Through the stratagems devised in the NSC, America is now embarking on a course of first strike, preemptive aggression. It has incorporated global commerce and the world's environmental future into national security, thus broadening the definition of national interests and what can officially trigger direct action. The Bush strategies reflect Condi's attitude that opposition must be met with overt strength, and strength must be used decisively. Condi believes in timely forceful action to protect America first; then secondly to give oppressed people of other countries the right to shape their destiny. When given a choice, Condi believes people wherever they may live will always choose freedom. In perhaps the most comprehensive national security directive in the history of the U.S. government, she helped outline what lengths establishing freedom of choice can take.

Coming from a different perspective, detractors of the Bush approach say intrusive actions executed behind the scenes for decades have now become clear public policy that will thwart the freedom they espouse to protect and move the lines of political morality to new lows. In wide ranging national strategies coupled with broad powers granted the president by Congress, personal freedoms of law-abiding citizens and freedom of the press are at risk of being trampled under the rush of seeking to destroy terrorism before any illegal actions have taken place. Likewise, financial safety nets Americans enjoy and the sanctity of American private enterprise may fall under the weight of U.S. policies bolstering the growth of international corporations. Many objectors worry legal lines dividing privacy and markets free from government intervention are being blurred. Opponents to related military action feel that peace can never come from waging war. Reason brings peace; war attracts more violent retaliation. And, as far as weapons of mass destruction are concerned, they say America needs to get its own house in order to cease proliferating such dangers.

Condi may have softened her viewpoint on the nation acting unilaterally and does not publicly name the foreign states dubbed "rogue." But to opponents of the broad preemptive nature of the National Security Strategy and National Strategy to Combat Weapons of Mass Destruction, she said emphatically, "It's important in statecraft to always be aware of the downside of action, and to try to mitigate any downsides that might come into being. Everyone understands that there are unanticipated consequences. But I think if you go through history you can make a very strong argument that it was not acting, or acting too late, that has had the greatest consequences for international policies—not the other way around."

POWER MATTERS

In honor of the heights of power to which Condoleezza Rice had risen in her life, she was bestowed with the prestigious NAACP President's Award in 2002. That was followed later in the year by a fabulous duet with classical cellist Yo-Yo Ma during the presentation of the National Medal of Arts Award in Constitution Hall in Washington. Their performance

Holding the President's Award, National Security Advisor Rice delivers her acceptance speech at the 33ᵈ Annual NAACP Image Awards Ceremony held in Los Angeles in 2002. In her speech, Rice thanked her parents for encouraging her to strive for success.

brought Condi's musical talent to the world stage. Those light-hearted rewards gave way in 2003 to the implementation of the foreign strategy to combat weapons of mass destruction. Condi, the woman who has often said her dream job is commissioner of the NFL, sat beside her commander-in-chief, (a far cry from the football field), as he ordered American and coalition forces to march to Baghdad, the capital of Iraq.

Some people asked why invade the country of Iraq, identified to be part of the "axis of evil," while leaving a similarly categorized country, North Korea, alone. To that question, Condi has responded that Japan, China, and Russia have strong interests in a peaceful solution to stopping North Korea's development of nuclear weaponry. President Saddam Hussein and his Iraqi regime have no such support from multiple nations traditionally recognized as superpowers. Although most countries have not approved of and only a few have offered military assistance for preemptive action to forcefully remove Iraq's leadership, the U.S. claims a coalition of nearly fifty nations backed the American-led invasion of Iraq. Their numbers, by the way, were less than that which supported the invasion of Afghanistan.

But to clarify the coalition of nations against the Saddam Hussein regime, Condi wrote in March 2003 that to their merit, the coalition has not failed to act in ways that meet their political tolerance and military or economic capabilities. The British joined forces with the United States in front line movement to secure Iraq, while the Australian navy provided gun support. Poles gained control of an offshore Iraqi oil rig. Danes, Czechs, and Slovaks offered specialized noncombatant expertise respectively in intelligence and biochemical detection and response. Assistance from other coalition members may be less direct and visible, but Condi believes in their own valued way all fifty nations helped win the war.

American officials say war is necessary because at stake is the peril of mass deaths from toxic biochemical weapons in Iraqi hands. Previously, weapons of mass destruction were allegedly used by Saddam Hussein's regime against Iranians in war and against adversarial Iraqis. The fear was that he would use them whenever seriously threatened or to expand his sphere of power in the Middle East. Condi further said that Saddam Hussein took billions of illegal oil profits that could have been used to purchase more weapons and foment terrorism in other countries. At least one terrorist training camp existed in northern Iraq and may have had connections to al Qaida. Condi also stated that Iraqis offered $25,000 to Palestinian parents of suicide bombers. To those atrocities add an alleged threat to kill the elder Bush during his presidency. What allows the national security advisor to sleep at night is knowing efforts in which she played a key role are underway to eliminate those dangers and that a comprehensive plan is in place to protect America's future while freeing the Iraqi populace being trampled under Saddam's feet.

In the first two weeks of the operation, more bombs were loosed to shake the Iraqi leadership into submission than in any previous war. The bombs were intended to achieve ferocious and penetrating devastation on military targets. They were accompanied by a massive ground assault unleashed in troop strength reminiscent of the tens of thousands in the Vietnam War. In marching to Baghdad, as many Allied men and women put their lives at risk to secure freedom for the Iraqi people and to curb terrorism on United States citizens.

Condi has been instrumental in fashioning the strategies for the new world order in this second Bush White House that is coming to understand that life never proceeds as planned. Rice and her colleagues in the Bush Cabinet are realizing that the world is too small to discount global opinion.

These are uncertain times for the leaders of this great nation and its people. The outcome of America's War on Terror, and the world view of America in the 21st century, are yet to be determined. But through all the uncertainty, one thing is certain: National Security Advisor Condoleezza Rice's unwavering support and trust for her president and for the idea of democracy.

1954   Born to Angelena and John Rice in segregated Birmingham, Alabama on November 14.

1957   Begins piano lessons with her mother and grandmother.

1960   Begins one year of home schooling.

1961   Parents mentor her through public school.

1965   First African American to integrate Birmingham Southern Conservatory of Music; moves to Tuscaloosa, Alabama.

1969   Moves to Denver, Colorado.

1971   Graduates St. Mary's Academy high school and completes first year of college.

1972   Changes university major from music to political science; Professor Josef Korbel becomes mentor.

1974   Graduates cum laude with a Bachelor of Arts degree and Phi Beta Kappa; enters master's program at University of Notre Dame; Professor George Brinkley becomes mentor.

1975   Receives Master of Arts degree in government studies from Notre Dame; begins post-graduate classes at University of Denver.

1977   Interns at the Pentagon.

1981   Graduates with a Ph.D. in international studies from University of Denver; receives fellowship from Stanford Center of International Security and Arms Control; Professor Coit Blacker becomes mentor; and becomes an assistant professor in political science.

1984   Publishes first book, *Uncertain Allegiance: The Soviet Union and the Czechoslovak Army, 1948 – 1963*; bestowed Walter J. Gores Award for Excellence in Teaching; foreign policy advisor for the Gary Hart campaign.

1985–1986   Hoover Institute Fellow.

1986   Publishes second book, *The Gorbachev Era*, coauthored with Alexander Dallin.

1986–1987   International affairs fellow on the Council on Foreign Relations; special assistant to the Director of the Joint Chiefs of Staff.

1987   Promoted to tenured associate professor of political science; Brent Scowcroft becomes mentor.

1989–1991   Appointed Director of Soviet and East European Affairs in the National Security Council; promoted to Senior Director; named Special Assistant to the President for National Security Affairs.

1991–1993   Returned to teaching at Stanford; Senior Fellow at the Hoover Institute where George Schultz becomes mentor.

1991–2001   Board member at Chevron Corporation.

1991   Joins the boards of TransAmerica Corp. and Hewlett-Packard; joins Aspen Strategy Group.

1993   Promoted to full professor in political science; appointed youngest, first female, first African-American provost at Stanford.

1994   Joins Board of Trustees at Notre Dame.

1995   Publishes third book, *Germany Unified and Europe Transformed: A Study in Statecraft* with Philip Zelikow; joins J.P. Morgan's Board of Directors; meets George W. Bush.

1997   Awarded National Exemplar at Notre Dame; inducted into American Academy of Arts and Sciences; serves on Federal Advisory Committee on Gender-Integrated Training in the Military.

1999   Joins Charles Schwab's Board of Directors; resigns as provost; becomes foreign policy advisor for George W. Bush's campaign.

2001   Sworn in as National Security Advisor to the president of the United States.

2002   Wins the NAACP Presidential Award; performs in concert with cellist Yo-Yo Ma; produces National Security Strategy of the United States and National Strategy to Combat Weapons of Mass Destruction.

ABC News. "Bush's Foreign Policy Guru Condoleezza Rice Veteran of Bush Administration." *abcNews.com.*

BET. "Condoleezza Rice: How Do You Like Her Now?" *bet.com,* Jan. 21, 2003.

BET. "Condoleezza Rice: Who is This Powerful Black Woman?" *bet.com,* Nov. 27, 2002.

Bundy, Beverly. "Condoleezza Rice's poise, power a gift from her parents." Knight Ridder/Tribune News Service, Jan. 29, 2002.

Bush, Pres. George W., Speaking on the National Security Strategy of the United States of America. Washington, D.C.: The White House. Sept. 17, 2002.

ChevronTexaco. "Condoleezza Rice, Newly Named National Security Adviser, Resigns From Chevron Corporation's Board of Directors." Chevron Press Release Archives. San Francisco, CA, Jan. 16, 2001.

CNN. "September 11: Chronology of terror." *CNN.com,* Sept. 12, 2001.

Crock, Stan. "Condoleezza, Rice National Security Adviser." *BusinessWeek online.* Washington, D.C., Feb. 11, 2002.

DeYoung, Karen and Mufson, Steven. "A Leaner and Less Visible NSC Reorganization Will Emphasize Defense, Global Economics." *Washington Post.* Washington, D.C., Feb. 10, 2001.

Feliz, Antonia. *Condi: The Condoleezza Rice Story.* New York: Newmarket Press, 2002.

Furtado, Cassio. "Bush, Caroso discuss Argentine economy, war on terrorism." Knight Ridder/Tribune News Service, Nov. 8, 2001.

FWN Select. "Bush will tell De La Rua Argentina must carry out zero deficit." *FWN,* 2001.

Hampton, Henry. *Eyes on the Prize: America's Civil Rights Years* video series. Atlanta, GA: Turner Home Entertainment, PBS Home Video: Blackside, Inc., 1995.

Hawkins, Denise. "Condoleezza Rice's Secret Weapon: How Our National Security Adviser finds the strength to defend the free world." *Christian Reader,* September/October 2002.

Hoover Institution. "Condoleezza Rice." *expandNATO.org,* 2002.

Kemper, Bob. "U.S., Russia close to deal on reducing stockpiles of nuclear weapons." Chicago, IL: Knight Ridder/Tribune News Service, Nov. 1, 2001.

Ketterman, Steve. "Bush's Secret Weapon." *Salon.com,* Politics 2000.

Kiefer, Francine. "At the table of war, a trusted voice of caution." *The Nation*, 2001.

Lehrer, Jim. "Condoleezza Rice." *Online NewsHour*, March 11, 2002.

Lemann, Nicholas. "Without A Doubt: Has Condoleezza Rice changed George W. Bush or has he changed her?" *New Yorker*, October 14 & 21, 2002.

NAACP News. "National Security Advisor Condoleezza Rice To Receive The President's Award." *NAACP.org*, Jan. 30, 2002.

People Weekly. "Condoleezza Rice: Right-Hand Woman (The 25 Most Intriguing People 2001)." *Time*, Dec. 21, 2001.

Ratnesar, Romesh. "Condi Rice can't lose George W. Bush's foreign-policy adviser is a future superstar. But can she save Bush from himself?" *CNN.com*, Sept. 20, 1999.

Rice, Condoleezza. *Acknowledge that you have an obligation to search for the truth.* Stanford University, CA: Stanford Report, June 16, 2002.

Rice, Condoleezza. *Aug. 1: Bush's Secret Weapon, Condi Rice's Convention Address.* Philadelphia, PA: *abcNews.com*, Politics Ready When You Are, 2000.

Rice, Condoleezza. "National Security Advisor Rice speaking on Protecting U.S. Infrastructure." Washington, D.C.: The White House. March 22, 2001.

Rice, Condoleezza. "'Our Coalition,' an Op-Ed from Dr. Condoleezza Rice." Washington, D.C.: The White House. March 26, 2003.

Rice, Condoleezza. "Press Briefing by National Security Advisor Condoleezza Rice." Washington, D.C.: US Newswire, Nov. 1, 2001.

Rice, Condoleezza. "Press Briefing By National Security Advisor Dr. Condoleezza Rice On Visit Of President Putin." Washington, D.C.: US Newswire, Nov. 15, 2001.

Rice, Condoleezza. "Walking in faith." Washington, D.C.: The White House, Aug. 27, 2002.

Robinson, James. "Velvet-glove forcefulness: Six years of provostial challenges and achievements." Stanford, CA: *Stanford online Report*, June 9, 1999.

Sammon, Richard. "Bush's Seasoned Team for Antiterror Campaign." *The Kiplinger Business Forecasts*, Sept. 14, 2001.

Taylor, Adrian. "New National Security Adviser of President elect George W. Bush." *TIMESWeb*, June 2000.

The Trotter Group. "National Security Advisor Condoleezza Rice, 1:00–1:55 p.m." Trotter Group Black Voices in Commentary, Nov. 3, 2002.

United Press International. "Now we wait." Washington, D.C.: UPI, Oct. 8, 2001.

United Press International. "Rice addresses African ministers." UPI, Nov. 7, 2001.

Warner, Margaret. "Rice on Iraq, War and Politics." *Online NewsHour*, Sept. 25, 2002.

The White House. *Biography of Dr. Condoleezza Rice: National Security Advisor.* Washington, D.C.: The White House, 2001.

The White House. "Press Briefing by National Security Advisor Dr. Condoleezza Rice." Washington, D.C.: *Whitehouse.gov*, May 16, 2002.

The White House. National Security Council, Washington, D.C.: The White House.

The White House. "National Strategy to Combat Weapons of Mass Destruction." Washington, D.C.: The White House, Dec. 2002.

Wilkerson, Isabel. "The Most Powerful Woman in the World." New York, NY: *Essence*, Feb. 2002.

Williams, Juan. *Eyes on the Prize: America's Civil Rights Years, 1954-1965.* New York, NY: Penguin Books, Blackside Inc., 1987.

Winfrey, Oprah. "Oprah talks to Condoleezza Rice." New York, NY: *O Magazine*, Feb. 2002.

"Acknowledge that you have an obligation to search for the truth," Commencement speech to Stanford University graduates June 16, 2002, *Stanford Report*, California.

Condi: The Condoleezza Rice Story by Antonia Felix, Newmarket Press, New York 2002.

"The Most Powerful Woman in the World." Isabel Wilkerson, *Essence*, New York, Feb. 2002, Vol. 32, Issue 10, p. 114, 11 p., 3 c.

"The National Security Strategy of the United States of America," The White House, President George W. Bush, Sept. 17, 2002.

"National Strategy to Combat Weapons of Mass Destruction," The White House, Dec. 2002.

"Oprah talks to Condoleezza Rice," *O Magazine*, Feb. 2002, Vol. 3, Issue 2, p. 118, (7).

"Rice on Iraq, War and Politics," Sept. 25, 2002 interview on *PBS Newshour* by Margaret Warner

The Trotter Group interview of National Security Advisor Condoleezza Rice, 1:00–1:55 p.m., 11/03/02, Trotter Group Black Voices in Commentary.

"Velvet-glove forcefulness: Six years of provostial challenges and achievements." James Robinson, Stanford [online] Report, California, Issue of June 9, 1999.

"Walking in faith." *Washington Times* with permission of White House, Aug. 27, 2002.

"Without A Doubt: Has Condoleezza Rice changed George W. Bush or has he changed her?" Nicholas Lemann, The *New Yorker*, October 14 & 21, 2002.

www.abcnews.go.com

www.cnn.com

www.du.edu

www.expandnato.org

www.nd.edu

www.pbs.org/newshour

www. seattlewebservices.com/rice (Condoleezza Rice 2008—Unofficial Website—RUN! CONDI! RUN!)

www.stanford.edu

www.tiesweb.org/interviews/rice

www.whitehouse.gov

Index

Index

Picture Credits

Gloria Blakely emerged on the literary book scene in 2002 with the biography of Danny Glover for Chelsea House's *Black Americans of Achievement* series. She later coauthored *Profiles of Great African Americans* and the *African American Heritage Perpetual Calendar* released in 2003 by Publications International, Ltd. Her contributions to literature have been recognized with appearances on radio and television. She writes on a variety of topics for such well-known magazines as *Essence, Heart & Soul, Pathfinders Travel,* and *Black Diaspora,* and has contributed to newspapers, including the *Philadelphia Sunday Sun,* the *Philadelphia Tribune,* the *Los Angeles Sentinel,* and the *Central Florida Advocate.*

Ms. Blakely, a graduate of the Howard University's honors program, is an active member of the Philadelphia Association of Black Journalists. She is listed among the up and coming children's book writers in *Something about the Authors* published by Gale services.